Event Sponsorship

This introduction to event sponsorship provides students with an essential understanding of the important role of sponsorship in an event, how this can be gained and successfully managed to the benefit of both the sponsor and sponsee.

The text starts with an investigation of the origins of sponsorship and then considers all important elements of events sponsorship management. It considers what sponsorship is; its history and evolution; what its marketing uses are; how it can be used efficiently; the benefits it can bring to an event; and how its results can be measured. It also considers other funding sources for events including government grants, crowd source funding and merchandising. To reflect changes in the way firms communicate with their customers, there is a strong focus on the use of social media, e-marketing and technology in sponsorship. The text uniquely considers topics of sponsorship from the perspective of both sponsor and sponsee (the event) to provide a holistic view of the sponsorship process.

Case studies are integrated throughout to show how both small and large scale events have successfully gained and used sponsorship as well as potential pitfalls to avoid. Learning outcomes, discussion questions and further reading suggestions are included to aid navigation throughout the book, spur critical thinking and further students' knowledge. *Event Sponsorship* is essential reading for anyone studying events management.

Ian McDonnell is a Senior Lecturer at University of Technology, Sydney's Business School. Ian's research interests lie in the areas of international tourism marketing, tour guides, tourism precincts, cultural tourism, special event management and special event sponsorship. He is a co-author and originator of the best-selling textbooks *Festival and Special Event Management*, translated into four languages and now in its fifth edition, and *Events Management* with Glen Bowdin.

Malcolm Moir is Head of Development at Sydney Festival. He has worked in the arts and events area since 1981 and held positions ranging from Box Office Co-ordinator to General Manager. Sponsorship, commercial development, government funding and philanthropy are his areas of speciality. He has worked for organisations including Opera Australia, Sydney Opera House, Opera New Zealand, Sydney Organising Committee for the Olympic Games, Powerhouse Museum and Sydney Festival, as well as many contract sponsorship assignments.

This book is a welcome addition to the literature on sponsorship. The authors provide a comprehensive and incisive insight into the world of sponsorship exploring its origins to the role it plays in the digital age. It will provide the reader with an eclectic mix of examples which clearly demonstrate the importance, relevance and significance of sponsorship to the events and marketing industry.

Claire Blanchard, Head of Marketing Tourism Events Management,
University of Chester

Event Sponsorship

Ian McDonnell and Malcolm Moir

Routledge
Taylor & Francis Group

LONDON AND NEW YORK

First published 2014
by Routledge
2 Park Square, Milton Park, Abingdon, Oxon OX14 4RN

and by Routledge
711 Third Avenue, New York, NY 10017

Routledge is an imprint of the Taylor & Francis Group, an informa business

© 2014 Ian McDonnell and Malcolm Moir

British Library Cataloguing in Publication Data
A catalogue record for this book is available from the British Library

Library of Congress Cataloging in Publication Data
McDonnell, Ian.
Event sponsorship / Ian McDonnell and Malcolm Moir.
  pages cm
Includes bibliographical references and index.
ISBN 978-0-415-53387-4 – ISBN 978-0-415-53388-1 – ISBN 978-0-203-11390-5
1. Special events – Management – Case studies.   2. Corporate sponsorship –
Case studies.   I. Title.
GT3405.M44 2013
394.2068 – dc23

2013016901

ISBN: 978–0–415–53387–4 (hbk)
ISBN: 978–0–415–53388–1 (pbk)
ISBN: 978–0–203–11390–5 (ebk)

Typeset in Frutiger
by RefineCatch Limited, Bungay, Suffolk

Printed and bound in Great Britain by
TJ International Ltd, Padstow, Cornwall

Contents

Contents

Illustrations

Tables

Figures

Case studies

Foreword

Sponsorship has come a long way in the last 20 years from being a relatively unsophisticated investment in an activity to a heavily scrutinised and debated element of the marketing expenditure of organisations.

While the literature on sponsorship is building there are few textbooks devoted to the subject, and the writers hope this book brings some of the contemporary literature together and provides useful information to students.

In the book there appear the terms Event Producer and Sponsee – these are used interchangeably and both refer to the party seeking sponsorship support.

Acknowledgements

Thanks to:

Jack Southwell, editor of Chapters 5–10
Alexandra Shehadie, Persephone Moir and Natasha Moir for their support
Adam Jeffrey and Fran Bartlett
Peter Larum and John Moore
Ian Jickell and Phil Gibson
John Elliott
Sarah Stahle
Caroline Yuen
Judith Craig and Nicola Pickavance

And all the individuals and organisations that have agreed to sponsor a property I was representing! – YOU KNOW WHO YOU ARE – THANKS!

Chapter 1

What is sponsorship?

Learning outcomes

After thoroughly reading and discussing the contents of this chapter, students will be able to:

- define and describe sponsorship from the point of view of both the sponsor and the sponsee (the property);
- explain how sponsorship fits into the marketing mix and the marketing communications mix;
- show an understanding of how sponsorship has evolved from the time of the Ancient Greeks;
- give convincing reasons for the exponential growth in sponsorship as a marketing communication medium over the past 20 years.

Introduction

This text has two aims: one is to be a functional textbook for students of sponsorship who are undertaking degrees or diplomas in marketing, and/or event, sport, or tourism management, and their lecturers/teachers. This book provides students of sponsorship with a sound working understanding of what is sponsorship, its history and evolution; what its marketing uses are, how it can used efficiently and effectively as a marketing medium; the benefits it can bring to an event; and how its results can be measured.

The other aim is for it to be a reference resource and guide for practitioners, both from the sponsor and the sponsee perspective. The word sponsee simply means the event property holder, and is used in the same way as the words 'consignor' – a person consigning or sending something, and 'consignee', the person to which the consignment is sent.

It therefore deals comprehensively with all the varied aspects of sponsorship, with a different aspect considered in each chapter. The chapter starts with learning outcomes and finishes with a chapter summary of salient points; and then discussion questions to help students apply and better comprehend the principles discussed. A case study that illustrates the sponsorship elements discussed in the chapter then follows, which also utilises similar discussion questions. These questions can be used to facilitate discussion by a class leader; or readers can simply use the questions to test their comprehension of the subject matter by formulating answers to these questions.

In terms of its use as a reference it is hoped that students will not sell the text into the second hand book market at the conclusion of the subject, but keep it as part of the nucleus of their professional library, proudly displayed in their office book case for use as a source of inspiration and guidance during their careers in marketing and management. And of course practitioners who have come from other disciplines, or who have been away from the academy for some time, can also use it as a source for ideas on how to construct effective and efficient sponsorship packages; or conversely use it to ensure that their sponsorship spend is both effective and efficient as a marketing communication medium.

The text is multi-perspective in that it addresses the topic from both the point of view of the sponsor, the sponsee and other stakeholders in the sponsorship process. And it takes the view that sponsorship is an integral part of an organisation's marketing mix, and must be integrated with all other elements of its integrated marketing communications mix.

As it is an academic text, all uses of other scholars' work are referenced using the usual academic referencing system, and the full list of references is shown at the end of each chapter.

What is the marketing mix?

Before the marketing mix can be described it is necessary to decide on what is 'marketing'. McDonald (2007) provides a worthwhile framework in which to discuss marketing by dividing the concept into two parts. He defines the marketing concept as implying that all of the activities of an organisation are driven by a desire to satisfy their consumers' needs; whereas the marketing function is the management of the marketing mix. The marketing concept in other words means that all of an organisation's efforts are used to satisfy consumer needs; however, this must be done profitably or the future of the organisation can be limited.

McDonald (2007) goes on to explain that marketing is a process for:

- defining markets (that is selecting target markets for the product, usually by geography – place of residence, and demography – age, gender, socio-economic status, and psyschographics – lifestyle;
- quantifying the needs of the customer groups in the target market (segments in marketing speak) – that is establishing the size and purchasing value of the target market segment(s);
- determining the value proposition (that is the mix of product features at a competitive price) to meet these needs;
- communicating these value propositions to the target market segments;
- monitoring the value being delivered.

The concept of the marketing mix was first introduced in 1960 by Professor E. Jerome McCarthy, when he put forward the idea that the mix consisted of four elements (or variables, now referred to as the four Ps): price, product, place and promotion (McCarthy 1960), which has been used ever since by marketers; and it is the management and manipulation of these four variables to achieve an organisation's objectives that make up a marketing manager's job.

The marketing mix has since been refined by one of the greats of academic marketing, Professor Philip Kotler, as the mixture of controllable marketing variables that the firm uses to pursue the sought level of sales in the target market (Kotler 1984). However, though many additional 'Ps' have been suggested by academic marketers over the years (people, physical evidence, process, for example; which are really just elements of the product P), the four Ps first suggested by McCarthy over 50 years ago are still applicable, and still used extensively.

Price alludes to the price charged for the good or service, and can be manipulated by marketers to gain a competitive advantage, provided of course that the costs of production are lower than the price charged to the consumer, over the long term.

Product covers the consumer need satisfying features of the good or service being offered to the consumer, and includes elements such as branding, service quality, the presentation of the product, its features and benefits, and its ability to satisfy consumer needs.

Place refers to the place where the product reaches the consumer, and refers to the distribution chain that gets the product from the producer to the consumer, usually via wholesalers and retailers. However, one huge change in the distribution of goods and services (another term for place) has been the digitalisation of the economy, which has resulted in the disintermediation of the distribution channel between producer and consumer. For example, airlines now sell most of their tickets direct to the consumer via their web site, rather than using the services of intermediaries such as travel agents.

Promotion refers to the marketing communication activities that an organisation carries out to influence the buying behaviour of its target market, in which sponsorship plays a role. To be effective and efficient, these marketing communications must be integrated, to ensure a consistent message is transmitted.

What are integrated marketing communications?

One of the authors of this text (McDonnell) has written extensively on this topic and a precis of his work on IMC (from Allen *et al.* 2011) is given below.

While the term integrated marketing communications has long been found in the marketing literature (see for example, James 1972; Shaw *et al.* 1981; Barry 1986; Linton and Morley 1995; Belch and Belch 2004; Nowak and Phelps 2005), its first use in the area of a leisure marketing activity was probably that of McDonnell (1999) who used the case of Australian leisure travel to Fiji and Bali to demonstrate how integrated marketing communications help achieve a tourist destination's marketing objectives. He proposed the intefrag marketing continuum, which in the case of Fiji and Bali showed that the closer an organisation's marketing was to the integrated end of the continuum (and further away from the fragmented end, hence 'intefrag') the more effective it would be.

As with the marketing of tourism products and other leisure services, so it is with using sponsorship of special events as a marketing communication medium. The more integrated the marketing communication, the more effective it will be in achieving an organisation's marketing objectives because potential consumers see and hear uniform, consistent messages, imagery and activities produced to satisfy needs that motivate them to purchase the marketer's product.

Smith and Taylor (2004) describe the marketing communications mix as consisting of:

- personal selling
- publicity
- merchandising
- advertising
- sponsorship
- word of mouth
- sales promotion
- exhibitions
- corporate identity
- direct mail
- packaging.

All of these elements can be effectively used by marketers of products that also use the sponsorship of special events as a communication medium. They state that integrated simply means that a unified message is consistently reinforced, when any or all of these communication techniques are used, which means that the messages are consistent and cohesive.

From another viewpoint, the American Association of Advertising Agencies defines integrated marketing communications (AAAA 2011) as:

> A concept of marketing communications planning that recognizes the added value of a comprehensive plan that evaluates the strategic roles of a variety of communication disciplines – general advertising, direct response, sales promotion, public relations (and sponsorship) – and combines these disciplines to provide clarity, consistency, and maximum communication impact.

Yet another view of IMC is that of Shimp (2003, p. 42), who considers 'all sources of contact that a consumer has [with the product] as potential delivery channels for messages and makes use of all communication methods that are relevant to consumers'. The underlying premise of Shimp's view is of course that all sources of contact have consistent messages, constantly reinforced with similar meanings. Though none of these definitions mention the various methods of using the Internet as a promotional medium (social networking sites, web sites and ticket distribution sites) it also applies to this medium.

From these definitions it can be seen that for marketing communications to be properly integrated they must have the qualities of being unified and consistent with all aspects of the product's marketing mix and clear in their message, which results from a co-ordinated management process. This is reinforced by Linton and Morley's (1995) claim that the advantages of integration (IMC) are consistency of message, more effective use of media, improved marketing precision, cost savings, creative integrity and operational efficiency – all laudable aims.

Masterman and Wood (2006) have a useful table that compares traditional marketing communications processes with IMCs, which summarises the advantages of using IMC in an organisation's promotion plan.

From this albeit brief foray into the world of marketing, it can be seen that sponsorship is one variable in an integrated marketing mix, which in turn is one of the four Ps of an organisation's marketing mix. Marketers manipulate this mix in order to achieve marketing objectives such as to achieve x units of product sales, or to increase market share in a particular market by x per cent, or to achieve x per cent growth in sales revenue. The key point to remember is that sponsorship does not happen in isolation from other aspects of the marketing mix, but is integrated into it to help achieve an organisation's marketing objectives.

Table 1.1 Comparisons

Traditional marketing communications mix	Integrated marketing communications mix
Each type of promotion has separate function; fragmentation of messages and imagery and therefore brand image occurs	All types integrated into one strategy: synergy occurs between various types – sponsorship and sales promotion for example
Process starts with the product	Starts with customer needs and how the product can satisfy these
Fragmented communication programmes	Unified, consistent programmes
Short-term objectives for each promotion campaign	Relationship and brand building objectives
Mass audiences	Targeted to product consumers and stakeholders
Each type of promotion has specialist practitioners	Integrated campaign co-ordinated by a marketer

Source: Adapted from Masterman and Wood (2006).

What is sponsorship?

Sponsorship has become a critical element in the integrated marketing communication mix of many private and public sector organisations. Among the different types of marketing communication (for example, public relations, advertising, personal selling, sales promotions and direct marketing), sponsorship is said to be one of the most powerful media now used to communicate and form relationships with stakeholders and target markets, according to Grey and Skildum-Reid (2003).

Although sponsorship may be attached to social causes and broadcast media such as television programmes as well as to special events, just about every public special event is now sponsored in some way. With the emphasis now on 'connecting with' rather than 'talking at' the marketplace, special event sponsorship can be an ideal way for marketers to create brand interaction with consumers and stakeholders.

In academic circles, sponsorship has been defined in various ways. For example, Getz (1997) describes it as companies or individuals who provide money, services or other support to events or event organisations in return for specified benefits.

Geldard and Sinclair (2004) on the other hand define it as the purchase of the, usually intangible, exploitable potential rights and benefits associated with an entrant, event or organisation which results in tangible benefits for the sponsoring company (image/profit enhancement).

Whereas Distinguished Professor John Crompton (who, by the way has written some of the more influential and persuasive academic articles on this topic) describes sponsorship as a reciprocal relationship that involves an organisation and a business engaging in an exchange that offers commensurate benefits to each entity (Crompton 1994). Figure 1.1 illustrates this reciprocal arrangement.

The key point raised by Crompton is that the relationship is reciprocal; that is both the sponsor and sponsee give some benefit and receive a benefit in return. This reciprocity is the essential difference between sponsorship and philanthropy, where the philanthropist expects no commercial benefit from his/her gift (except perhaps a warm feeling of good being done).

The British sponsorship company BDS Sponsorship (2012) uses this as their definition of the concept: Sponsorship is a business relationship between a provider of funds, resources or services and an individual, event or organisation which offers in return rights and association that may be used for commercial advantage in return for the sponsorship investment. This definition highlights again the reciprocal relationship involved in sponsorship, and the importance of the commercial nature of the relationship.

The well-known American sponsorship consultancy IEG defines sponsorship as a cash and/or in-kind fee paid to a property (typically a sports, entertainment, event, or organisation) in return for the exploitable commercial potential associated with that property (in Cornwell et al. 2005). The in-kind fee referred to means that instead of paying in cash the sponsor pays in product. For example, if an airline was a sponsor of an event their in-kind services would be airline tickets to the value of the sponsorship.

IEG also state that sponsorship spending by companies in North America fell slightly in 2009 (by 0.8 per cent) but still amounted to a spend of $16.51 billion. This amount can be compared with a spend of $10.2 billion in 2003 and $13.4 billion in 2006 (IEG 2006; 2009). However, the global spend on sponsorship grew to a new record

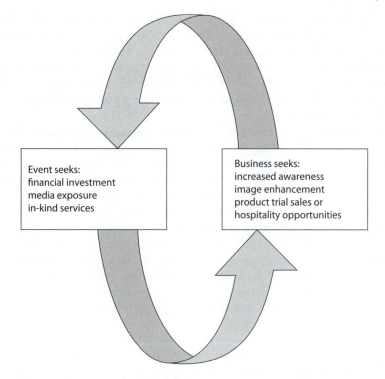

Figure 1.1 The exchange relationship in event sponsorship
Source: authors.

of $48.7 billion, a 5.2 per cent increase over 2010 (IEG, 2012a) and they forecast that spending on sponsorship in the Asia Pacific region will grow by 4 per cent in 2010 to $10.4 billion (IEG, 2012a).

And finally, that great authority, the *Oxford English Dictionary* (2012a) defines 'to sponsor' as 'to pay, or contribute towards, the expenses of a radio or television programme, a performance or other event or work, *spec.* in return for advertising space or rights', and 'sponsorship' as 'the state of being a sponsor; the office of a sponsor'. While the word sponsorship was used as early as 1809, in the sense of one person sponsoring, or looking after the interests of another, it was first used in its current meaning in 1935, when a journalist stated 'the sponsorship of the Philadelphia Symphony Orchestra by Philco' (*Oxford English Dictionary* 2012b).

After reviewing these academic and practitioner definitions it can be seen that sponsorship is a strategic marketing communication investment by the sponsor, not a donation (philanthropy) or a grant (a one-off type of assistance). This means that management of special events of all types (sports, special events, festivals, arts and performers) must view sponsorship as a working business partnership between the sponsor and the sponsee (the event or property as the modern marketing lexicon calls it). Sponsors are marketers who expect to see a direct impact on their brand value (enhanced awareness and imagery) and a consequential potential for increased sales.

Heineken sought brand exclusivity for its beer and increased sales through its Rugby World Cups sponsorship, and Kia seeks heightened worldwide brand awareness and product features of its cars as a result of its sponsorship of the Australian Open tennis major. An interesting example of contra (or in-kind support) instead of cash used in sponsorship is Australian national youth radio Triple J and music video Channel V's sponsorship of the popular music festival the Big Day Out. The sponsor receives greater brand recognition and the event receives promotion on the radio and cable TV media to which their target market listens. The important aspect of these sponsorship examples is that the sponsor seeks a return on their investment that is superior to the returns from an investment in other forms of promotion, or is complementary to their other marketing communications.

In the case of public sector sponsors, some kind of social marketing result is usually sought (for example, a greater awareness of water conservation or the dangers of drink driving). Another example is the UK's National Lottery, which spent 66 million pounds on sponsoring the London Paralympic Games in order to support Britain's Paralympic athletes and to encourage this sporting activity at the grass roots level.

Creating a successful event that can generate cash or contra from sponsors means establishing a reciprocal relationship between the organisation providing the sponsorship (corporate, media and/or government) and the special event. However, it also means an emotional connection must be made with those consumers targeted by both the event and its sponsors. This three-way relationship that underpins the success of sponsorship is illustrated in Figure 1.1. Sponsors use events to emotionally tie their product or service to a market segment that identifies with the event and consequently identifies with the sponsor's product.

But the key point to always keep in mind is that sponsorship is part of the integrated marketing communications mix, which is a component of the marketing mix, described in the next section.

Trends in sponsorship

The chapter now discusses a number of trends, including the need for more innovative and flexible marketing media, which underpin the rising popularity of sponsorship. As Meenaghan (2005) points out, sponsorship as a marketing communication medium has increased a great deal over the last 20 years; probably twentyfold.

The reasons for this increase were itemized 20 years ago by Meenaghan (1991) as:

- government policies on the advertising of tobacco and alcoholic products;
- escalating costs of media advertising, particularly television;
- new opportunities because of increased leisure activity;
- greater media coverage of sponsored events; and
- inefficiencies in traditional media – clutter and zapping.

Twenty years later Shimp (2010) found these reasons for the rapid increase of sponsorship:

- avoid clutter – that is the multitude of messages found on radio and television that inhibit potential consumers taking note of the message;
- response to changes in consumers' viewing-time switching, recording of programmes, on demand TV, that make advertisements less effective and efficient;
- the relationship between an event and the brand of the sponsor can enhance the brand's equity by increasing its awareness and enhancing its image;

- the ability of sponsorship to tightly target specific geographic areas or demographic groups.

Another significant trend in the digital era is the importance of You Tube as a medium. If a sponsorship message can be made to go 'viral' (that is the link to the You Tube video is spread from viewer to viewer) the reach of the sponsorship is greatly extended, which increases the effectiveness of the sponsorship. However, the way that is made to occur depends on the creativity of the sponsor and their agency responsible for the creative aspects of the sponsorship.

The growth in the use of sponsorship sales agencies is another. Sales agencies are brokers that bring together the property (sponsorship speak for the event) and a potential sponsor. IEG (2012b) report that sales agencies accounted for 10 per cent of the total number of sponsorship deals in 2011, up from 9 per cent in each of the previous two years and 7 per cent in 2008. As sponsorship increases in value and importance as a marketing communication medium this trend will only increase, bought about because events (or properties) outsource their property's sponsorship potential to experts.

Another trend of significance to both sponsors and sponsees is what IEG (2011) calls post event fulfillment reports in which the event reports to the sponsor on what they have delivered and how successful they were in meeting the requirements of the sponsor. These reports can also be given midway through the event's season – sporting or theatrical – which enables the sponsor to tweak the sponsorship activity if necessary, and confirms to the sponsor that the deal is worthwhile. Additionally, the use of third parties who can conduct independent research on the communication objectives gives the report credibility. As well, the use of specialised software such as Turnkey's Activator assists in providing a consistently formatted and useful report that can only cement ongoing relationships between the event (property) and the sponsor.

These trends (and many other issues of significance to sponsorship managers) will be discussed in the following chapters of the book.

A short history of sponsorship

A few scholars have made an attempt at establishing the origins of sponsorship, and most agree that it originated in the classical Greek and Roman era, *circa* 2000–3000 years before the present. For example, Desbordes and Tribou (2007) indicate that Julius Caesar and other Roman emperors of that era sponsored gladiatorial contests.

According to the University of Pennsylvania's Museum of the Ancient Olympics, they were as dependent on sponsorship as are the current Olympics. In the ancient Olympics, Greeks marketed their athletic heroes by poets composing odes about them, and sculptors made images of the victorious athletes (Penn Museum 2012). Swaddling (2002) claims that the stadium and site used by the ancient Olympic Games was surrounded by concession stands selling food, drink and souvenirs, and sculptors and poets hawked their wares – so not a huge difference to the marketing activity that surrounds major sporting events today.

The reasons for that sponsorship were, according the *University of Chicago Encyclopedia* (2012), similar to the reasons why governments to this day sponsor large scale sporting and artistic events: to add prestige to and add to the favourable reputation of the emperor (or government) by providing what the Roman historian Juventus labelled *panem et circenses*, bread and circuses. And in the present day media pundits can still be heard to claim that government sponsorship of special events is merely providing bread and circuses to placate the masses, so Juventus' words still echo down the millennia.

The next recorded instance of sponsorship in the form that it is known today was by the Medicis, a wealthy and powerful Florentine family of the fifteenth and sixteenth centuries, of the artists of the Renaissance period in Europe. Allen *et al.* (2011) describe the sponsorship of the Medici family, and in particular that of Cosimo the Elder and his grandson Lorenzo the Magnificent. They sponsored painters, sculptors and poets such as da Vinci, Donatello and Botticelli, who were and still are an integral part of Western civilization and culture. It is reasonable to assume that they did this for the same reason that governments sponsor museums and art galleries in every part of the world – to encourage artists to produce fine work and to have a place that can show these works in order to both assist in generating goodwill towards them from a defined group of peple, to generate awareness and acceptance of their policies and to enter-tain their constituents and other stakeholders with hospitality centered on these artistic endeavours.

Dolphin (2003) concurs with this and goes on to claim the word sponsorship itself derives from the ancient Greek *horigia*, which is a combination of the words *horos* (the dance) and *iigoumai* (I direct or I lead). The individual who led or paid for the festival/dance was the *horigos* or sponsor (Quester and Thompson 2001). However, this seems highly unlikely, as dictionary.com gives its derivation as being from the seven-teenth century and coming from the Latin *sponsus* meaning guarantor. The *Oxford English Dictionary Online* agrees with this etymology and states that it was first used in the meaning of 'one who pays, or contributes towards, the cost of a broadcast programme or other spectacle, especially in return for commercial advertisement', in 1931 by one P. Dixon in the magazine *Radio Writing*, viz., 'the sponsor wants a dramatic type of program and is willing to spend one thousand dollars a week for the program'.

Collins and Vamplew (2002) make the fascinating observation that sponsorship of sporting and other special events has been linked with the brewing industry and its distributors for centuries. They make the point that by the sixteenth century, and perhaps much earlier, the British village pub or ale house was the producer of village sports as diverse as cricket, quoits, boxing, wrestling, foot racing and many other events such as dances that could in turn attract crowds to their establishment – a very early form of sponsorship. And it is also of interest to note that beverage companies are still major sponsors of these sorts of activities, but now use the medium of tele-vision to communicate their messages.

Desbordes and Tribou (2007) outline the growth of sponsorship in this way:

1861   Spiers and Pond (a Melbourne hotelier and restaurateur) sponsored the tour of Australia by the English cricket team – as an aside this dynamic duo also introduced railway catering on their return to Britain; though there is some discussion whether they were sponsors or promoters – see Haigh (2012).

1864   Sports clothes retailer and champion cricketer John Wisden sponsored the publication of the cricketing bible *Wisden Cricketers' Almanack*, and of course obtained naming rights that continue to this day, long after the sponsorship ceased.

1887   Michelin Tyres sponsor by contra (the supply of tyres) cycle races in France.

1920s   The advent of radio as an entertainment medium led to the 'sponsorship' of various programmes, which generally included the name of the sponsor in the programme's title. Programmes such as *The Champion Spark Plug Hour* and *The Firestone Hour* were exemplars of the genre.

This timeline shows that sponsorship is not just a contemporary phenomenon but has been part of the marketing communications mix for many years.

However, it was upon the introduction of television broadcasting immediately after World War II (though it was first broadcast in England shortly before the war, but ceased on its commencement) in the UK and the USA that sponsorship became a more significant part of the marketing communications mix. Moreover, it was the introduction in the developed world of colour television into the majority of homes in the 1960s (1970s in Australia) that commercial sponsorship as it is known today became an integral part of the marketing communication mix. Meenaghan (1991) illustrates this by stating that in the UK, in 1970 expenditure on sponsorship was a mere £4 million, but by 1980 had grown to £35 million, and by 1990 to £288 million, 70 times greater than the 1970 spend. Meenaghan (1991) also gives details of how quickly companies adopted sponsorship as a marketing communication medium – from 700 odd companies in 1981 to over 2,000 in 1988, and now the $48 billion spent on sponsorship worldwide.

Summary

This chapter has introduced sponsorship by defining what it is, and how it fits into an integrated marketing communications mix, and an organisation's marketing mix. These concepts have been defined and explained. The key point to remember from the sponsor's perspective is that sponsorship is one of many media that can be used to effectively communicate with a target market; and it must be integrated (that is be consistent and unified with the organisation's entire marketing communications).

From the perspective of the property (the sponsee), it must be never forgotten that the sponsorship that it has attracted is a marketing communication medium for the sponsor and the property must do all in its power to enhance and facilitate this communication. By doing this, ongoing relationships between sponsor and sponsee can be strengthened, and the sponsorship retained for many years.

Discussion questions

1   Explain the discrepancy between the different etymologies of the word sponsorship given in this chapter.
2   Why should marketing communications be integrated?
3   Why are beverage companies enthusiastic users of sponsorship?
4   How does sponsorship differ from advertising?
5   List the reasons why post-event fulfillment reports are necessary to maintain and retain sponsors.

Case study 1.1

Lessons from sponsorship of the Sydney 2000 Olympics

As already noted in this book, the rise of the sponsorship industry has been quite dramatic over the past 30 years. In 1980, US$300 million was spent globally on sport sponsorship while three decades later this amount had increased to US$46 billion. Along with this commercial growth has been the increasing academic interest in sponsorship research. One area of research that has often been neglected, though, has been that of sponsorship renewal: in other words, the attempt to understand why some sponsors renew their commercial partnerships with sport properties while others do not. A recent study by Morgan and Frawley (2011), however, has started to fill this research gap. The study explored the sponsorship of an Olympic Games from the viewpoint of a major stakeholder, in this case the host National Olympic Committee (NOC), and specifically whether a sponsorship legacy was achieved post-Games for the host NOC. Morgan and Frawley (2011) in particular examined the internal and external characteristics that influenced the host NOC sponsors in either renewing or terminating their commercial partnerships with the host NOC. To achieve this research objective the Sydney 2000 Olympic Games was selected as the central case study, with interviews undertaken with 15 senior executives representing both the sponsors and the host NOC, in this case the Australian Olympic Committee. The following discussion provides an overview of a section of the findings that emerged from the research.

Four key themes arrived from the analysis of the interview data. They were: the positive and negative legacies to emerge from hosting the Sydney 2000 Olympic Games for the AOC; sponsor attraction to the Olympic Movement; sponsor relations with the AOC; and the geographic and cyclic nature of Olympic sponsorship. The first of these themes is addressed in detail below.

Within the legacy theme three key areas emerged. First, the positive impact hosting the Games had on the AOC and the sponsors that sought to enhance their image based on this impact. The data showed that the Sydney Games helped the AOC raise its profile in domestic and international markets. As outlined by a study respondent: 'I think it [the Olympics] put the AOC in a better light. It certainly bought Olympic sport to another level in Australia. Therefore, it made it more attractive for sponsors to be involved [with the AOC].'

Second, it was noted some negative consequences emerged from the hosting of the Games for the AOC. For instance, while the profile of the AOC increased in the lead up period to the Games for the AOC, sponsor attraction post-event was not an automatic conclusion. For instance, the AOC projected before the Games that for the 2001–2004 period they would raise AUD 60 million; however, they were only able to achieve half that amount. According to a senior AOC official interviewed for the study: 'we started the quadrennial in 2001 hoping to raise AUD 60m in sponsorship . . . based on the Sydney Olympic experience. We ended up with AUD 28m for the four-year period, less than half.' In 2001, major sponsors of the Sydney Olympics, Visa and Coca-Cola, ceased their association with the AOC despite their continued involvement with the Olympic Movement through their sponsorship contracts with the International Olympic Committee (IOC). Thus for some IOC sponsors the benefits of a partnership with an NOC diminishes rapidly once the hosting of the Games is complete. In the immediate period post-Sydney 2000 sponsorship attraction to the AOC was unclear. As outlined by McGuire (2001, p. 34):

> maybe it's just that six months after the event it is still too soon for some companies to make a decision or maybe there is still a general Olympic-fuelled malaise in sport marketing, or maybe there is still a lingering dis-satisfaction among sponsors surrounding their treatment.

The consequence of this sponsorship downgrade was a negative impact for the funding of the Australian Olympic team preparing for the 2004 Athens Olympic Games. For instance, in 2003, AOC president, John Coates stated: 'people have had Olympic saturation. While we have more sponsorship money than we had for the Atlanta Games [1996] it hasn't been without its pain' (Morgan and Frawley 2011, p. 225). As outlined above, the sponsorship target for 2001–04 was AUD 60 million; however, only AUD 28 million was achieved for the period. The above points indicate that, even with the success of the Sydney 2000 Olympic Games and the AOC's heightened visibility, the corporate interest in the AOC post-2000 was overly optimistic.

Third, it was noted that post-2000 the sponsorship environment had changed significantly in Australia. Respondents argued that the huge financial investments made by some sponsors of the Games resulted in a different market post-Games and that the experience gained by sponsors and their staff resulted in a more sophisticated market. As outlined by a respondent, the sponsorship market gathered 'a level of expertise and understanding that perhaps it did not have before' (Morgan and Frawley 2011, p. 229). Therefore while the AOC did not receive a financial boost in the form of increased sponsorship investment post-Sydney 2000, the sponsorship industry itself gained momentum in Australia after the Games. For instance, a report conducted by the Commercial Economics Advisory Service of Australia indicated that 2001 was a steady year for sport sponsorship and despite the aftermath of the Sydney Olympics, sport sponsorship investment across Australia actually increased by 2 per cent.

Dr Stephen Frawley and Dr Ashlee Morgan

Case study discussion questions

1 What caused the AOC to think that they could attract AUD60 million in sponsorship after the 2000 Olympics?
2 Why did interest in sponsorship of the Australian NOC reduce so significantly?
3 What could the Australian NOC have done to improve their sponsorship offer?

References

AAAA (2011) *Integrated Marketing Communications*. Accessed at www.business-dictionary.com/definition/integrated-marketing-communications-IMC.html

Allen, J., O'Toole, W., Harris, R. and McDonnell, I. (2011) *Festival and Special Event Management*, 5th edn, Wiley Australia, Brisbane.

Barry, T. (1986) *Marketing: An Integrated Approach*, The Dryden Press, Chicago.

Belch, G. and Belch, M. (2004) *Advertising and Promotion: An Integrated Marketing Communications Perspective*, 6th edn, McGraw-Hill, Boston.

BDS Sponsorship (2012) *The Definition of Sponsorship*, available at www.sponsorship.co.uk/in_sponsorship/in_sponsorship.htm (accessed 12/1/12).

Collins, T. and Vamplew, W. (2002) *Mud, Sweat and Beers: A Cultural History of Sport and Alcohol*, Berg, Oxford.

Commercial Economic Advisory Service of Australia (2012) *Sponsorship of Sport 2001*, available at http://users.tpg.com.au/ceasa/spons.html

Cornwell, T., Weeks, C. and Roy, D. (2005) 'Sponsorship-linked marketing: Opening the black box', *Journal of Advertising*, vol. 34, no. 2, pp. 21–42.

Crompton, J. (1994) 'Benefits and risks associated with the sponsorship of major events', *Festival Management and Event Tourism*, vol. 2, issue 1, pp. 65–74.

Desbordes, M. and Tribou, C. (2007) 'Sponsorship endorsements and naming rights', in Beech, J. and Chadwick, S., eds, *The Marketing of Sport*, Pearson Education, Harlow.

Dictionary.com, available at http://dictionary.reference.com/browse/sponsor

Dolphin, R. (2003) 'Sponsorship: Perspectives on its strategic role', *Corporate Communications*, vol. 8, issue 3, p. 173.

Geldard, E. and Skinner, I. (2004) *The Sponsorship Manual*, 2nd edn, The Sponsorship Unit, Melbourne.

Getz, D. (1997) *Event Management and Event Tourism*, Cognizant Communication Corporation, New York.

Grey, A. and Skildum-Reid, K., (2003) *The Sponsorship Seekers Toolkit*, McGraw-Hill, Sydney.

Haigh, G. (2012) 'Cricket running itself out in chase for the fast buck', *The Australian*, available at www.theaustralian.com.au/news/sport/cricket-running-itself-out-in-chase-for-the-fast-buck/story-fnb58rpk-1226249726714

IEG (2006) *IEG Sponsorship Report*, available at www.sponsorship.com/IEG/files/fc/fcbe683b-d2a8–4f0b-9b35–121a86ab3a2b.pdf

—— (2009) *IEG Sponsorship Report*, available at www.sponsorship.com/IEG/files/fc/fcbe683b-d2a8–4f0b-9b35–121a86ab3a2b.pdf

—— (2011) *Best Practice: Post-event Fulfilment Reports*, accessible at www.sponsorship.com/iegsr/2011/10/11/Best-Practices-Post-Event-Fulfillment-Reports.aspx

—— (2012a) *IEG Sponsorship Report*, available at www.sponsorship.com/IEG/files/fc/fcbe683b-d2a8–4f0b-9b35–121a86ab3a2b.pdf

—— (2012b) *The Growing Popularity of Sponsorship Sales Agencies*, accessible at www.sponsorship.com/iegsr/2012/01/09/Sponsorship-Sales-Agencies-Grow-In-Popularity.aspx

James, B. (1972) *Integrated Marketing*, Penguin, Harmondsworth.

Kotler, P. (1984) *Marketing Management: Analysis, Planning and Control*, Prentice Hall International, London.

Linton, I. and Morley, K. (1995) *Integrated Marketing Communications*, Butterworth Heinemann, Oxford.

Masterman, G. and Wood, E. (2006) *Innovative Marketing Communications: Strategies for the Events Industry*, Elsevier, Oxford.

McCarthy, E. J. (1960) *Basic Marketing: A Managerial Approach*, R. D. Irwin, Homewood, IL.

McDonald, M. (2007) *Marketing Plans: How to Prepare Them, How to Use Them*, 6th edn, Elsevier Butterworth Heinemann, Oxford.

McDonnell, I. (1999) 'The intefrag marketing continuum: A tool for tourism marketers', *Journal of Travel and Tourism Marketing*, vol. 8, no. 1, pp. 25–39.

McGuire, M. (2001) 'Once bidden, twice shy: Olympic backers back off', *The Australian*, 2 March, p. 34.

Meenaghan, T. (1991) 'Sponsorship: Legitimizing the medium', *European Journal of Marketing*, vol. 25, no. 11, pp. 5–10.

—— (2005) 'Evaluating sponsorship effects', in Amis, J. and Cornwell, T., eds, *Global Sport Sponsorship*, Berg, Oxford.

Morgan, A. and Frawley, S. M. (2011) 'Sponsorship legacy and the hosting of an Olympic Games: The case of Sydney 2000', *Journal of Sponsorship*, vol. 4, no. 3, pp. 220–235.

Nowak, J., and Phelps, J. (2005) 'Conceptualising the integrated marketing communications phenomenon: An examination of its impact on advertising practices', in Kitchen, P., de Pelsmacker, P., Eagle, L. and Schultz, D. E., eds, *A Reader in Marketing Communications*, Routledge, New York.

Oxford English Dictionary (2012a), available at www.oed.com.ezproxy.lib.uts.edu.au/view/Entry/187377

—— (2012b) available at www.oed.com.ezproxy.lib.uts.edu.au/view/Entry/187381

Penn Museum (2012) *The Real Story of the Ancient Olympics*, available at www.penn.museum/online-exhibits/516-the-real-story-of-the-ancient-olympic-games.html

Quester, P. and Thompson, B. (2001) 'Advertising and promotion leverage and arts sponsorship effectiveness', *Journal of Advertising Research*, vol. 41, no. 1, pp. 33–47.

Shaw, R., Seminik, R. and Williams, R. (1981) *Marketing: An Integrated Analytical Approach*, South Western Publishing, Cincinnati.

Shimp, T. (2003) *Advertising, Promotion and Supplemental Aspects of Integrated Marketing Communication*, 6th edn, Thomson, Ohio.

—— (2010) *Advertising, Promotion and Other Aspects of Integrated Marketing Communications*, 8th edn, Cengage Learning, Mason, OH.

Smith, J. and Taylor, J. (2004) *Marketing Communications: An Integrated Approach*, 4th edn, Kogan Page, London.

Swaddling, J. (2002) *The Ancient Olympic Games*, University of Texas Press, Austin.

University of Chicago Encyclopedia (2012) 'The Roman Gladiator', available at http://penelope.uchicago.edu/~grout/encyclopaedia_romana/gladiators/gladiators.html

Chapter 2

Sponsorship as a marketing medium

Learning outcomes

After reading, discussing and comprehending this chapter, readers should be able to:

- explain how sponsorship works as a marketing communication and distribution channel (or medium);
- describe its advantages over other forms of marketing communication;
- depict its value to the sponsor as a marketing communication medium;
- establish its ability to target market segments efficiently and effectively.

Introduction

Before embarking on this chapter's theme it is necessary to establish what is meant by communication, in a marketing sense. Duncan and Moriarty (1998, p. 2) define it as 'the human activity that links people together and creates relationships', and they go on to explain how it is at the heart of not only marketing activities, but a wide range of social, political, economic and psychological actions. They argue that effective communication, because of its meaning-making, plays a unique (and fundamental) role in building brand relationships. And this book argues that building brand relationships and its consequential commercial activity is the *raison d'être* for sponsorship activity.

Many twentieth-century scholars have tried to model the process to better explain how communication works. One of the first was Lasswell (1948), whose model is shown in Figure 2.1 below.

Lasswell's model, interestingly, followed the ancient Greek philosopher Aristotle (1994) as its starting point for examining this issue; however, he adds to Aristotle's original concept the element of medium, or the channel that is used to communicate the message. His model has the advantage of being simple and making it easy to understand the linear process of communication, but it omits two vital elements: 'noise' and 'feedback'. Noise refers to all the extraneous activities that are occurring in the receiver's environment, which may impact on the effectiveness of the communication. Feedback refers to any communications that the receiver may send to the sender, regarding the content of the message.

This omission of 'noise' was remedied in the Shannon and Weaver (1949) model shown below in Figure 2.2.

This model, unlike the others discussed, was developed in the Bell laboratories – a manufacturer of communication devices such as telephones – to better understand how machines can communicate with each other, though it has obvious use for modelling human communication. It uses the now standard communication model elements of information, namely: source – the sponsor or marketer in this case; encoder – the way the sponsorship message is worded or pictured; channel – the medium or media used to transmit the message; receiver/decoder – the target market for the message; and destination – an appropriate response from the target market. The insight that Shannon and Weaver (1949) provided was the element of 'noise'.

They were referring to noise that could interfere with the transmission between apparatus, such as static, but in marketing terms 'noise' refers to anything that can inhibit the intended recipient from receiving the message. Noise can be as diverse as

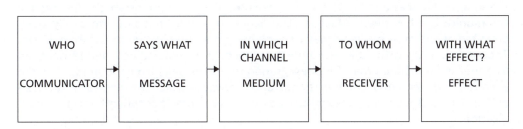

Figure 2.1 Lasswell's communication process
Source: Lasswell (1948).

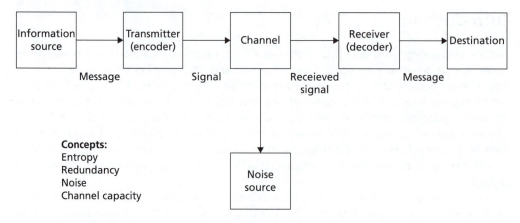

Figure 2.2 The Shannon–Weaver mathematical model, 1949
Source: Shannon and Weaver 1949.

the myriad other marketing messages being transmitted in the receiver's environment, other activities that are occupying the receiver's attention, or simply a lack of interest in the message. This 'noise' is often referred to as 'clutter' in the marketing communication lexicon; and a common expression in this field is 'to cut through the clutter', which means a message that has the intended affect on the recipient by cutting through the 'noise' in the receiver's environment.

The work of Shannon and Weaver (1949) influenced Wilbur Schramm, who influenced greatly the thinking on how communication works. His model introduces the elements of feedback and field of experience.

Field of experience refers to the orientation or attitudes the communicants have to each other. In marketing terms this means how complete is the understanding that the marketer has of their target market – the wants, needs and desires that can be satisfied by consumption of the sponsor's product, and the attitudes that the target market has towards the sponsor's product.

Feedback refers to any actions that the recipient takes that can inform the sender of the effectiveness of the message. In face-to-face communication this feedback can, for example, consist of avoidance of eye contact, looking away or other signs of disinterest in what the sender is communicating, or alternately it can be enthusiastic agreement manifested by smiling, nodding or encouraging words. In a marketing communication environment, the feedback could be close to immediate, if the marketer used some form of research at the sponsored event to establish what recipients thought about the sponsorship messages, or delayed if they use sales figures to establish whether the communication has been effective. The Schramm model has now generally been accepted as the most effective way of explaining how human communication works. Though it is noteworthy that Schramm uses 'encoder, signal and decoder' rather than 'channel' in his model. What this does is separate the message from the sender (i.e. the encoder), the medium or channel (signal) and the way in which the message is received and understood (decoder), all of which are necessary to use to ensure effective communication.

Schramm's (1954) model can be adapted to a marketing communication such as sponsorship thus:

- Sender – the firm or organisation that is communicating with a target market by the use of a sponsorship.
- Encoder – is distilling the message creatively so that it will resonate with the target market and achieve the behaviour change required.
- Encoder's field of experience – this refers to the understandings and knowledge of the target market that the sender and encoder have.
- Signal – choosing which medium is to be used to transmit the message.
- Decoder – the message is received by one of the target market's senses (sight, hearing, touch, smell or taste).
- Noise – any activity that may stop the intended recipient effectively receiving the message.
- Decoder's field of experience – the recipients' previous experience with a product or brand of this type, or the feelings and emotions that the recipient may have towards the brand.
- Feedback – any change in buying behaviour or attitude towards the brand that the recipient has.

This model has rather cleverly been used by Duncan and Moriaty (1998) as the basis for their parallel communication and marketing process model, shown in Figure 2.3. For marketers involved in sponsorship – both sponsor and the event property (the sponsee) – this model shows how the marketing mix is heavily reliant on effective two-way communication between the marketer and the consumer.

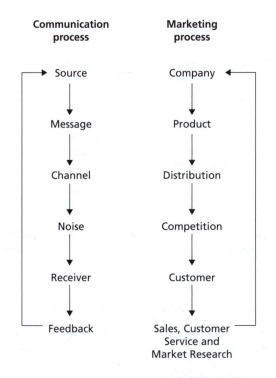

Figure 2.3 Parallel communication and marketing processes
Source: Duncan and Moriaty (1998).

They propose the view that all elements of the marketing mix communicate with the consumer: marketing communications both planned and unplanned – word of mouth, mentions in the media; the product or service itself – its design and performance; and the service standards surrounding the product; the product's price that can communicate value or quality; and the distribution channel used also can communicate a product feature. These aspects send messages to the consumer. And of course, effective sponsorship can play a significant part in the communication of suitable messages, as well as all the other communications the product's marketing mix sends.

They also make the significant point that effective communication makes for effective relationships between the product and the consumer, which in turn enhances the value of a brand. Brand value comes from, according to SDR Consulting (2012), the premium that a brand can charge over a competitor offering a similar product. This ability to charge a premium price for a similar product is acquired from:

● the intangible product attributes and image features that potential consumers have of the brand; and
● the customer target market that is willing to pay a premium for a particular brand.

Keller and Lehmann (2003) have developed a model that neatly explains the processes that can form 'brand value', which is shown in Figure 2.4.

As can be seen from this fairly self-explanatory model, it is the firm's marketing activity (that of course includes integrated marketing communications, of which spon-

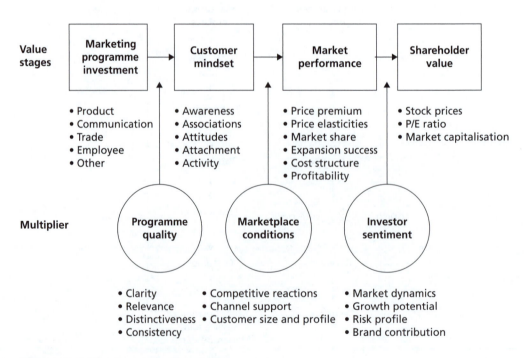

Figure 2.4 The brand value chain
Source: Keller and Lehmann (2003).

sorship is a part) that provides the driver that produces a brand image in the minds of consumers. The key aspect in this model in terms of sponsorship activity is the marketing programme quality. As Keller and Lehmann (2003) point out, what multiplies, or in other words, increases the quality of the marketing process in consumers' minds, are the elements of clarity, relevance, distinctiveness and consistency.

One method of doing this is for marketers to use sponsorship as a channel (marketing communication medium) to increase brand performance that contains these elements, and that is the next topic to be discussed.

Sponsorship as marketing communication channel

There are a large number of channels (or media) that marketers can use to communicate with a chosen target market: newspapers, magazines, other print media, radio, television, the World Wide Web, packaging, personal selling, public relations, publicity and outdoor sites (billboards, posters, sides of taxis and buses). All have their place depending on the target market. For example, marketers of a fast moving consumer good, say female hair products, that has a mass market would choose a different channel from marketers of niche products such as golfing equipment.

Table 2.1 below shows these various channels and the uses. To fully comprehend the use of these media as a marketing communication channel, two concepts must first be explained: reach and frequency.

Reach refers to the number of individuals or households in the target market that will see the marketing communication enough times to make an impact on their buying behaviour. The key here is 'target market'. It is a waste of resources if a marketing communication is seen by tens of thousands of people if the target market receivers are measured in the hundreds. Frequency refers to the number of times the potential consumers receive the marketing communication. The minimum frequency is usually considered to be three or four times within a month, though Krugman (1972), an advertising practitioner, recommends three as the optimum effective and efficient

Table 2.1 Various channels of communication

Channel (medium)	Benefits	Weaknesses
Daily newspapers	Flexibility in production; timely; good coverage of a geographical area; message receivers can re-read and keep the message for future reference.	Lots of 'noise'; not well-targeted to a market; short life; low production quality (but improving); increasing competition from digital media.
Sunday newspapers	Read in more detail due to more leisure time of readers.	As for newspapers.
Magazines (specialised)	Highly targeted market; good demographic selectivity; long life.	Tend to be expensive on cost per target market scale; long lead time.
Trade and specialist press	Tightly targeted.	Used only in business to business marketing.

Table 2.1 Continued

Channel (medium)	Benefits	Weaknesses
Internet banner ads	Cost effective as pay per click; flexibility in message; simple to change message when circumstances change.	Clutter (noise).
Word of mouth	Cost effective; most believable of all marketing communications.	Difficult to generate; social media can be an effective channel.
Social media	Cost effective; can act like word of mouth communication.	Difficult to control, can prove an embarrassment if the campaign goes wrong.
Television	Can quickly give credibility to a brand; wide market coverage; conveys a message with sight, sound, motion, builds brand images; pay TV offers access to niche markets.	Difficult to target effectively; lots of 'noise'; expensive production costs; quickly forgotten.
Radio	Low cost per thousand (cpm) listeners rates; low production costs.	High 'noise' (clutter); no shelf life; easily forgotten.
Cinema	Opportunity for high production values; works in well with TV advertising; good geographical targeting; can be targeted to a particular demographic.	Cost of production high; quickly forgotten; viewers annoyed that they have to wait for the film to start.
Outdoor	Billboards or advertisements on public transport are seen by a lot of consumers; creativity can be employed on message.	Can be expensive on a cpm of target market basis.
Direct mail (post)	Can be addressed by name and personalised; easy to measure effectiveness of campaign – number or response to offer; little noise.	Expensive if not tightly targeted.
Direct email	Cost effective provided data base of email addresses is valid.	Spoilt by unsolicited messages (spam).
Sponsorship	Many.	Some.

Source: adapted from Kotler *et al.* (1998); Professional Advertising (2005); PowerHomeBiz (2012).

number, and this number is the generally accepted industry minimum. However, Moorey-Denham's (2007) experience in online promotion shows that a concentrated media exposure over 24 hours has a greater impact on product purchase or consideration than a campaign spread over a number of weeks.

The cost of marketing communications is usually calculated as the cost per thousand (usually expressed as cpm – cost per *mille*, Latin for one thousand). That is, the cost of the medium (channel) is divided by the number of thousand receivers of the message.

As can be seen in Table 2.1, marketers have many channel options at their disposal when they wish to communicate with their market. The role of the property owner (the sponsee) is to convince the potential sponsor that the communication channel with their target by sponsorship of their property is more effective and efficient than the use of any other media. The role of the marketer is to evaluate this relative to the use of other channels to establish if sponsorship is the more effective and efficient marketing communication channel to use. In this context, effective means being able to achieve the measureable objectives of the marketing campaign – sales revenue; market share growth; image enhancement; or profit. Efficient means using the minimum of resources – money, time, human resources – to achieve the maximum possible outcome – the required change in sales, market share, profit or image.

By using the Schramm model of communication, the advantages of using sponsorship as a communication channel from the perspective of the sponsor can be established. The first and probably the most salient advantage is that of *desired market targeting*. This refers to the decoder's field of experience, which can be receptive to the proposition put in the encoded signal that is the sponsorship.

But first it must be established by what is meant by the phrase target market. This simply means that group of customers whom the organisation (the sponsor) wants to communicate with. These groups can be segmented by:

- Demographics – age group, gender, education, income group.
- Geographics – place where consumption or purchase takes place.
- Psychographics – lifestyle, interests, cultural sets.
- Decision makers – those who make the purchasing decision.
- Behavioural – aligning customers by product usage: light, medium, heavy or by loyalty to the brand.
- Distribution – where customers purchase or consume the product.

(Olsen 2006)

Vodaphone, for example, could have a target market for a particular product that is predominantly male, educated, aged between 30 and 50, medium to high income, and interested in a particular genre of music. All market oriented organisations have a target markets that are segmented using the criteria shown here.

So then for music loving adults who are fans of more mature popular music acts, properties such as music festivals are an obvious channel, and Vodaphone a suitable sponsor. The Isle of Wight Festival, which caters to just this market and featured at the 2012 festival a line-up that included Tom Petty and The Heartbreakers, Elbow, Pearl Jam, Biffy Clyro, Bruce Springsteen and the E Street Band, and Noel Gallagher's High Flying Birds. The sponsors in 2012 were Ray-Ban, manufacturers of hip sun glasses and spectacles; Strongbow, manufacturers of alcoholic cider; Absolute Radio, a classic rock Internet radio station that targets the more mature popular music lover; and Vodaphone, a mobile phone company. All of these products have a target market that is congruent with the target market of the Isle of Wight Festival (Isle of Wight 2013).

The Big Day Out is an Australian popular music festival that targets 16–30-year-olds, and again the sponsors are congruent with that market – Radio JJJ, the Australian Broadcasting Commission's popular music radio station, and V, a pay TV music channel. Both these organisations feel that the sponsorship enables them to communicate with their target market in an effective and efficient manner as the message receivers are in the required demographic and psychographic set and are likely to respond to the sponsors' messages.

This shows that a key advantage of sponsorship as a marketing communication medium is that messages can be sent more effectively and efficiently to their desired receiver because every person receiving the message is of the desired target market and noise is kept to a minimum.

Another advantage is *image enhancement*. An organisation may want to show to its target market that it is community minded and not merely a profit generator. The sender (the sponsor) is encoding a signal that the sponsor's organisation is assisting the sponsee, which in turn may assist the message receiver. The receiver then decodes that signal in a positive way, and the image of the sponsor is thereby enhanced. For example, Surf Lifesaving Australia is a symbol of Australianness, and very well-regarded by the great majority of Australians. Its sponsors – DHL, a large logistics and freight carrying company; Westpac, one of the big four Australian banks; Telstra, the Australian telecommunications giant; and the Australian government's Department of Health and Ageing – use this sponsorship purely to enhance their image as a caring corporate citizen, and in the case of the Department of Health and Ageing to encourage safe practices when exposed to the sun (Australian for life 2013).

In the United Kingdom, the Royal National Lifeboat Institution (RNLI) has a similar iconic status. It is interesting to note that they do not refer to sponsors but to corporate partners. However, these corporate partners are sending the same image enhancement signals as the sponsors of Surf Lifesaving Australia (RNLI 2013a). For example, one of the RNLI's corporate partners is Yamaha, the Japanese manufacturer of outboard motors. As the UK regional manager of Yamaha said:

> It's great to be able to give something back to the RNLI while at the same time offering a benefit to our customers with this free membership package. As boaters we all rely on the fact that the RNLI will come to our aid if required when at sea, even in treacherous weather conditions, and this partnership will help support the RNLI and its fundraising activities.
>
> (RNLI 2013b)

This message brings the brand name Yamaha to its target market, and enhances its image as a company that cares about its customers' safety.

Another advantage is *brand awareness*, which can be defined as the extent to which a brand is recognised by its target market, and is correctly associated with a particular product. Brand awareness is of course more important in the early stage of a brand's life in a particular market. It is usually expressed as a percentage of the target market that is aware of the brand and its product features.

Depending on the property, sponsorship can be used to spread brand awareness internationally. A perfect example is that of Thai Singha beer, that according to the Manchester United web site 'has been quenching the thirst of beer drinkers in all corners of the world' (Manutd 2013). As it was only introduced into the UK in 2009, it was a brand with which few British beer drinkers were familiar.

The beer company (or more likely its advertising agency) decided that sponsorship of Manchester United FC was an effective method of raising brand awareness, as Manchester United FC fans and followers are congruent with the target market of Singha beer internationally. It encodes a signal using this sponsorship that it is a beer that is enjoyed in all parts of the world, and particularly with Thai food. The sponsorship message is then decoded by the receiver (the target market) who may then try the product at their next visit to a Thai restaurant. The main advantage of the sponsorship is that again 'noise' is minimised as there are no other conflicting messages being received by the consumer, its target market becomes aware of the brand and its attributes, and feedback comes from measurement of changes in sales volume.

Another purpose of sponsorship is *shaping of consumer attitudes* towards the sponsor's product. The classic example of this is the sponsorship by tobacco companies of sporting teams and events, until tobacco advertising was banned in the 1990s in most of the developed world. For example, in Australia, the Sydney and New South Wales rugby league competition was sponsored by Winfield, a well-known brand of cigarettes manufactured by British American Tobacco. The message that 'Winfield' supported the sport that smokers in Sydney and NSW enjoyed and watched either live or on TV, was delivered via this sponsorship, which manifested itself as the Winfield Cup, the prize for the successful team in the competition. This then made the target market's attitudes to the brand more positive. The encoder's field of experience gleaned from market research of the target market helped in producing messages that the receiver would decode in a positive fashion for the brand. This sponsorship was effective, as Winfield became the largest selling brand in that market (Wikipedia 2013). And of course the cigarette brand was associated with sport and its positive impact on the health of those who partook of exercise, which attempted to make consumers disregard the health consequences of smoking.

Yet another of sponsorship's advantages is its role in *product differentiation*. Many branded products have similar characteristics, particularly fast moving consumer goods such as soft drinks. Take Coca-Cola, a pleasant and very popular carbonated beverage. It differentiates itself from its many competitors not on price, or any other marketing variable, but on its brand, which is differentiated from its competitors by its sponsorship activity. For example, it was a major sponsor of the London 2012 Olympics, and gave these reasons for this:

> Coca-Cola has supported the Olympic Games since 1928, making us the longest continuous supporter of the Olympic Movement. We are a business, and so part of the reason for our sponsorship is to build awareness for our brands and the wide choice of quality and refreshing drinks we offer consumers. We sell a range of drinks at all Olympic venues during the events. Coca-Cola also shares the Olympic Movement's vision of connecting people with sport, and we are committed to promoting active, healthy lifestyles and increasing participation in sport at every level. In addition without the support of Coca-Cola and the other Worldwide Sponsors, as many as 170 of the 200 National Olympic Committees would be unable to send athletes to compete.
>
> (Coca-Cola 2013)

But as well as the stated brand awareness reason, discussed above, it also differentiates Coca-Cola from its competitors – Coke is the soft drink that helps to enable many of the great sporting events in the world to occur, which puts the Coke brand 'top-of-mind' amongst consumers. It does this by the use of a coded message – Coke is the drink of the Olympics – that adds to and reinforces the receivers' field of experience, which in turn sustains and reinforces the brand awareness of Coca-Cola.

Conclusion

Schramm's communication model, though now quite old, is indeed a useful model for analysing how communication works, and is just as useful in analysing marketing communications such as a sponsor using a sporting, artistic, cultural or any other type of special event as a channel (or medium) to send encoded signals to its target audience. This chapter has explained how this occurs and the advantages that accrue from this process.

The next chapter examines these advantages in some depth.

Discussion questions

1 The Schramm communication model is now quite old. Is it still valid? Why or why not? Are the other more useful models available? This web site may help your thinking – google 'communication models – images'.
2 What did Schramm mean by field of experience? How can this concept be used by a sponsor to enhance sponsorship activity?
3 How does 'noise' affect sponsorship marketing communications? How can it be minimised?
4 What causes conflict between the sender's field of experience and the receiver's? What actions can the sender take it ensure that their knowledge of the receiver's field of experience is congruent with their own?
5 Is the Duncan and Moriaty model of the Parallel Communication and Marketing Processes a useful tool for sponsors? If so, why? If not why not?

Case study 2.1

Jersey jackpot: FC Barcelona

For European football clubs, the signing of jersey sponsorship deals involve enormous sums of money and garners tremendous media interest. Now a top target for sponsor companies, jersey sponsorship – or the right to place a brand name across the chest of the playing strip – attracts multi-million-euro investments. Within the top six European professional leagues, total annual income of football jersey sponsorship doubled from 2001 to 2011, reaching over 470 million euros (SPORT+MARKT 2010). Manchester United and Liverpool FC generate the highest revenue from jersey sponsorship, boasting deals with AON and Standard Chartered worth 23.6 million euros each (SPORT+MARKT 2010).

Whilst virtually all football clubs in Europe have long sold jersey sponsorship rights, Futbol Club Barcelona (FC Barcelona), have renounced this revenue generating possibility. From the founding of the club in 1899 up until 2006, the FC Barcelona jerseys never displayed a sponsor's logo. The club and the fans prided themselves on their 'clean' playing strip, which to them symbolised the purity of sport and focused attention on the identity of their club. In 2006 this changed.

What transpired, though, was a highly unusual strategy. Whereas logos and insignia on playing strips normally involve corporate sponsorship and large financial investment, FC Barcelona donated their jersey advertising rather than selling it. In a stunning example of corporate social responsibility (CSR), the club signed a five-year partnership with UNICEF to help raise awareness and funds for children affected by HIV and AIDS. This agreement included the placement of the UNICEF logo on their jersey set. FC Barcelona also agreed to donate 1.5 million euros annually over the five-year period to help fund UNICEF projects (Fundació FC Barcelona 2012).

FC Barcelona's alliance with UNICEF reinforces the club's vision of community engagement and its slogan *mésque un club*, or 'more than a club'. Rather than seeking a lucrative sponsorship agreement, FC Barcelona prioritised its social engagement role and its image of moral leadership. This commitment to helping the impoverished children of the world has had positive ramifications for the FC Barcelona brand.

This case exemplifies the notion of brand image transfer. In the past this has predominantly been discussed in terms of the brand of the sport being transferred to the sponsor company. However, the influence of brand image is increasingly being recognised as a two-way exchange process. As such, the association with an organisation, be it a corporate sponsor or charitable entity, bears influence on the commercial image and civic reputation of the sport club within the marketplace. It is reasonable to assume that FC Barcelona's support for UNICEF provokes the flow-on of positive consumer perceptions instilled by the UNICEF brand, to the brand image of the club.

The initial agreement between FC Barcelona and UNICEF ended in 2011. The club extended the partnership, renewing for a further five-year period. The commitment from FC Barcelona continues, with the annual payment of 1.5 million euros to fund UNICEF projects. However, the UNICEF logo has now been moved to the back of the jersey, with FC Barcelona selling jersey sponsorship rights to the Qatar Foundation, a private non-profit organisation. Representing the largest football jersey sponsorship deal in Europe, the Qatar Foundation will pay 30 million euros each year, for a five-and-a-half year period ('Barcelona sign' 2010).

This change of focus raises a number of issues. In the capitalist business environment, with its current economic turbulence and uncertainty, financial sustainability is increasingly crucial for all organisations, with football clubs being no exception. Within this complex context, the intangibility of brand image for sport organisations makes its impact difficult to evaluate in financial terms. As such, the underlying question is: What creates more value?

Does the financial revenue obtained through selling sponsorship rights outweigh the positive brand enhancement associated with charitable donations? Or is brand image more beneficial, potentially creating flow-on effects and revenue generation in other areas? Despite FC Barcelona's continuing commitment to UNICEF, has the recent sale of the front of its jersey sponsorship undermined the CSR image of the club? Although the immediate financial gains are clearly in favour of selling jersey sponsorship rights, the flip side might be that enhancing brand image through CSR initiatives has greater long-term benefit for the brand. In this case study, could it simply be that FC Barcelona has captured the positive associations with the UNICEF brand, but can no longer resist the lucrative jersey sponsorship market? This case underscores the ever increasing commercialisation of sport and the upward financial pressures associated with running European football, with its extraordinarily large player salaries.

Case study discussion questions

1   Are there any other examples of a sponsee (the property) being a sponsor in the way that FC Barcelona sponsors UNICEF?
2   Has FC Barcelona now achieved the best of both worlds in remaining a sponsor of UNICEF, and selling their jersey rights for a very large sum? If so, why? If not, why not?
3   The Barcelona FC strip can show either the UNICEF logo or the Qatar Foundation logo (see www.fbcbarcelona.com). What advantages does the Qatar Foundation (www.qf.org.qa/) get from the large amount of money it pays for the sponsorship?
4   What is the encoded signal that the Qatar Foundation is sending to its target market? Does it reinforce its current field of experience of the Qatar Foundation?
5   What is the Qatar Foundation's target market? Why does the Foundation want to talk to them using this channel (medium)? This may help: www.qf. org.qa/news-center/fcb-en.

Dr Ashlee Morgan

References

Aristotle (1994), translated by Roberts, W., *Rhetoric*, Massachusetts Institute of Technology Classics, available at http://classics.mit.edu/Aristotle/rhetoric.html

Australian for Life (2013) accessible at www.sls.com.au

'Barcelona sign huge sponsorship deal' (2010, 10 December) CNN. Retrieved 21 March 2012 from http://edition.cnn.com/2010/SPORT/football/12/10/football.barcelona. sponsorship.qatar/index.html

Coca-Cola (2013) 'Why does Coca-Cola sponsor the Olympic Games?' available at www.coca-cola.co.uk/faq/olympic-games/why-does-coca-cola-sponsor-the-olympic-games.html

Duncan, T. and Moriarty, S. (1998) 'A communication-based marketing model for maintain relationships', *Journal of Marketing*, vol. 62 (April), pp. 1–13.

Fundació FC Barcelona (2012) 'Partnership with UNICEF'. Retrieved 21 March 2012 from http://foundation.fcbarcelona.com/projects/detail/card/partnership-with-unicef

Isle of Wight (2013) accessible at www.isleofwightfestival.com/

Keller, K. and Lehmann, D. (2003) 'How do brands create value?' *Marketing Management*, May/June, pp. 27–32.

Kotler, P., Bowen, J. and Makens, J. (1998) *Marketing for Tourism and Hospitality,* 2nd edition, Prentice Hall, NJ.

Krugman, H. (1972) 'Why three exposures may be enough', *Journal of Advertising Research*, vol. 12, no. 6, pp.11–14.

Lasswell, H. (1948) 'The structure and function of communication in society,' in Bryson, L., ed., *The Communication of Ideas*, Harper, NY, accessed at http://communicationtheory.org/lasswells-model/

Manutd (2013) 'Official sponsors Singha', accessible at www.manutd.com/en/Club/Sponsors.aspx?sponsorid={2B6C7989–8153-435D-B460–251E07116B41}

Moorey-Denham, S. (2007) 'Frequency of exposure is key for online ads', *New Media Age*, accessible at www.nma.co.uk/frequency-of-exposure-is-key-for-online-ads/35138.article

Olsen, E. (2006) *Strategic Planning for Dummies*, John Wiley and Sons, Chichester and New York, available at http://my.safaribooksonline.com/book/strategy-business-planning/9780470037164

PowerHomeBiz.com (2012) 'Choosing the right advertising for your small business', accessible at www.powerhomebiz.com/vol118/admediums.htm

Processional Advertising (2005) 'Using advertising media more effectively', accessible at www.myprofessionaladvertising.com/Using%20Media%20More%20Effectively.htm

RNLI (2013a) 'How to support us', available at http://rnli.org/howtosupportus/howweuseyourmoney/Pages/how-you-helped-last-year.aspx

—— (2013b) 'RNLI announces new partnership with Yamaha', available at http://rnli.org/NewsCentre/Pages/RNLI-announces-new-partnership-with-Yamaha.aspx

Schramm, W. (1954) 'How communication works', in W. Schramm, ed., *The Process and Effects of Mass Communication*, University of Illinois Press, Urbana, pp. 3–26.

SDR Consulting (2012) 'Measuring brand value', available at www.sdr-consulting.com/branding3.html

Shannon, C. and Weaver, W. (1949) *The Mathematical Theory of Communication*, University of Illinois Press, Urbana.

SPORT+MARKT (2010) 'European jersey report: Premier League jersey leader in Europe', press release. Retrieved 21 March 2012 from www.sportundmarkt.com/en/press/press-releases/2010–10–28.html

Wikipedia (2013) 'Winfield cigarette', available at http://en.wikipedia.org/wiki/Winfield_%28cigarette%29

Chapter 3

The marketing benefits to the sponsor

Learning outcomes

After reading, discussing and comprehending this chapter, readers should be able to:

- list and describe the marketing benefits that can accrue to a sponsor from an effective sponsorship programme;
- explain the marketing benefits that can accrue to a firm because of its sponsorship activities.

Introduction

Chapter 1 showed that sponsorship is a reciprocal process, in which the event property (the sponsee) receives a consideration in return for benefits accruing to the sponsor. This chapter discusses in some depth these advantages (or benefits); knowledge of which will enable a sponsee to maximise the benefits to a sponsor, and for the sponsor to maximise the worth of the sponsorship.

The benefits discussed are:

- brand awareness;
- image enhancement;
- target market specific audiences;
- media coverage;
- hospitality and entertainment for clients;
- client data base additions;
- sales promotions;
- product placement;
- product experience;
- product sales opportunities;
- sales promotion;
- reinforcement.

Each will be discussed in turn.

However, to give some underpinning theory to the discussion, the observations of Crompton (1996) are an excellent starting point, who begins by listing the possible benefits that may come from sponsorship of an event, which are shown in Table 3.1. These are similar to the benefits shown above, albeit expressed slightly differently. But what Crompton does show is that the desired benefits can be categorised into four main requirements.

Crompton (1996) makes the valid point that one of these categories (product trial or sales opportunities) is of a tactical nature (a tactic to make product sales at the event), whereas the other three are more strategic in nature – to encourage potential consumers to be aware of the product and then ultimately purchase it. However, if the sponsorship is structured correctly it should result in positive outcomes in all four categories. For example, a firm producing an up-market clothing line may sponsor a theatrical production at a leading capital city theatre. Such a sponsorship would enhance brand awareness of its product, and enhance the product brand image among its target audience, give opportunities for theatregoers to purchase the product at a discount, and give opportunities for distributors and retailers to be entertained at the production.

Figure 3.1 shows the AIDA model of consumer decision making, which Crompton (1996) uses as the starting point for his theory of how sponsorship works. The AIDA concept was first postulated by E. St Elmo Lewis, a nineteenth-century American marketer (provenmodels 2013). It was further reinforced by the pioneering work of Lavidge and Steiner (1961) who postulated that the hierarchy-of-effect buying stages are these:

The marketing benefits to the sponsor

1 At the bottom of the steps stand potential purchasers who are completely *unaware of the existence* of the product or service in question.
2 Closer to purchasing, but still a long way from the cash register, are those who are merely *aware* of its existence.
3 Up a step are prospects who *know what the product has to offer*.
4 Still closer to purchasing are those who have favourable attitudes toward the product – those who *like the product*.
5 Those whose favourable attitudes have developed to the point *of preference* over all other possibilities are up still another step.
6 Even closer to purchasing are consumers who couple preference with a desire to buy and *the conviction* that the purchase would be wise.
7 Finally, of course, is the step which translates this attitude into actual *purchase*.

These seven stages have been further refined into the four shown in the AIDA model shown in Figure 3.1. Kotler (1988) agrees with this refinement and suggests the differences in the two models are merely semantic.

The AIDA model shown in Figure 3.1 has been compared to the hierarchy of effects model by Crompton (1996) and the result shown in Table 3.2. As can be seen, the differences are just semantic, and AIDA has the big advantage of being easy to remember; after all it is the name of a very famous opera.

Table 3.1 Possible benefits arising from sponsorship

1. Increase awareness	(a) Create awareness of a new product
	(b) Increase awareness of an existing product in new target markets
	(c) Bypass legal prohibition on television advertising imposed upon tobacco and liquor products (though is no longer an option in many developed countries because of legal restrictions).
2. Image enhancement	(a) Create an image for a new product
	(b) Reinforce the image of an existing product
	(c) Change public perceptions of an existing product
	(d) Counter negative or adverse publicity
	(e) Build pride among employees and distributors for the product
	(f) Assist employee recruitment.
3. Product trial or sales opportunities	(a) Offer product trial to potential new customers
	(b) Induce incremental sales increases through promotional give-aways, coupon tie-ins
	(c) Create on-site sales opportunities
	(d) Promote a different use of an existing product
	(e) Reinforce the image of an existing product.
4. Hospitality opportunities	(a) Develop bonding with key customers, distributors and employees
	(b) Develop in-house incentive opportunities.

Source: Crompton (1996).

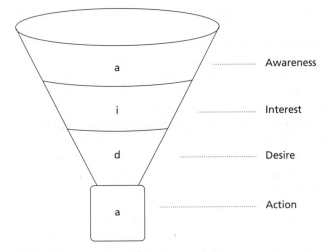

Figure 3.1 The AIDA sales funnel model
Source: St Elmo Lewis, 1898.

These four stages can be defined thus:

- Awareness means that the potential consumer goes from not knowing of the product's existence to being aware that it exists, and having some knowledge.
- Interest means that the potential consumer has gone from being merely aware of the product to having some interest in its attributes that can satisfy their needs; which usually results in a positive image of the product being formed.
- Desire means that the product is now wanted, or at least on a short list of products to be purchased that can satisfy their needs.
- Action of course means that the consumer decides to take an action that will result in either their owning the product or a decision to reject the offering.

Crompton (1996) brings in another element of the model that is relevant to the marketing communication's role of sponsorship – that is reinforcement, which can be defined thus:

- Reinforcement means that the consumer's loyalty to the product is confirmed, as is the belief that they have made a correct purchase decision.

Table 3.2 Relationship between two models of buying behaviour

AIDA stages	Hierarchy of effects stages
Awareness	Unaware; Aware Knowledge
Interest	Like the product Preference
Desire	Conviction
Action	Purchase

Source: Adapted from Crompton, 1996.

The marketing benefits to the sponsor

By using this model to underpin the sponsorship marketing communication process, the sponsor can plan activities that will facilitate the desired outcomes. This is illustrated in Figure 3.2, which shows the product adoption process (AIDA + R) (Reinforcement) model on the left and the sponsorship benefits on the right.

The variations in the arrow type (curved, thin, fat) represent the stage in the adoption process that the sponsor is influencing. For example, generating brand awareness in a long established and well-known brand is a waste of marketing resources, and is only applicable to new products being introduced into a market. The thin lines represent actions taken to further interest and increase desire among consumers who are aware of the product, while the fatter lines represent activities that can reinforce or consolidate attitudes towards the product amongst existing consumers.

What this means is that marketers seek different benefits from sponsorship, depending on the knowledge and understanding of their product's position in the market. An excellent example of this is Kia's (the Korean car manufacturer) sponsorship of prestigious sporting events around the world. When the Kia product first came to Australia in early 2002 they were an unknown auto brand. They then became the sponsor of the Australian Open Tennis championship, one of the five major world

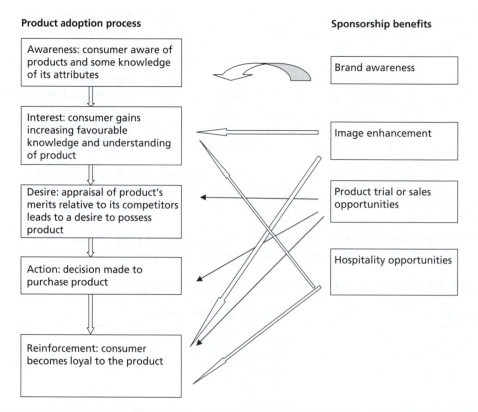

Figure 3.2 The potential roles of sponsorship in sponsoring the product adoption process
Source: Crompton, 1996.

tennis tournaments, taking over from its long-term sponsor Ford (McIlwraith 2012). Interestingly they did not claim naming rights as Ford had, but were content with the major sponsor title. This brand awareness sponsorship was effective as they have doubled their market share in the ten years of their sponsorship (McIlwraith 2012). Now that they are much better known in the Australian marketplace, the sponsorship benefits sought become more image enhancement, brand reinforcement and hospitality opportunities for distributors and other major stakeholders.

Now that the theoretical underpinnings are in place, each of the benefits listed previously are now discussed in some depth.

Brand awareness

Brand awareness simply means the extent to which a target market is aware of a brand's existence, and the ability of its attributes to satisfy their needs. In the early stages of a brand's introduction into a market, the major role of the promotion P is to increase this. As Kia realised, when a new product is introduced into a market the first marketing step is to increase brand awareness. When that has been achieved the next steps in the product adoption process can effectively take place.

And from effective brand awareness comes from what Oh (2002, p. 136) calls customer value, defined as 'a customer's perceived preference for and evaluation of those product attributes, attribute performances, and consequences arising from use that facilitate (or block) achieving the customer's goals and purposes in use situations' – an important step to get the consumer from the aware stage to the interest stage of the AIDA sales funnel.

For effective brand awareness to occur, the property (sponsee) must ensure that the messages relayed by the sponsorship raise awareness of both the brand and its product attributes. This means that the sponsor and property need to work together to ensure not only that consumers become aware of the brand name but also are aware of the need-satisfying attributes of the brand. A negative example of this is the sponsorship of the Manly Sea Eagles in the Australian National Rugby League by the Russian Internet security and anti-virus company KaSperSky. Even though the Manly strip has the brand name in large letters on its front, very little information regarding the product and its attributes is given either at Manly's home ground or in any other media. The only way that a link can be made to their product attributes is a link on the Manly web site to the KaSperSky site, but as very few know what the KaSperSky product is, it is unlikely that many potential consumers will make that effort.

Brand image

Brand image is defined by Gwinner and Eaton (1999, p. 47) as 'perceptions about a brand as reflected by the brand associations held in memory', and these come from many sources, such as consumer experiences of the brand, experienced or perceived product attributes, relative pricing, marketing communications, packaging, images of typical brand users, and usage occasion. Gwinner and Eaton (1999) state that brand awareness is enhanced by image transfer from the property to the sponsor, and can be done both by sponsorship of events, mainly sporting, and by celebrity endorsement. In the same way that a celebrity has a 'meaning' – defined as what a celebrity represents to the consumer – a sports team or sports event has a similar 'meaning', and that is what is transferred by the sponsorship. For example, polo is very prestigious sport, and the 'official supplier' (a sponsorship paid for with goods, known as contra or in kind sponsorship) is La Martina, a very up-market Argentinean clothing and polo apparel store – see La Martina (2013) for details of their operations. Another sponsor of Polo is Cartier, the exclusive jeweller, as the sponsor of the Coronation Cup held between Great Britain and other international polo teams. Both these firms seek the benefit of image enhancement form the sponsorship of the sport of polo.

Gwinner (1997) is of the view that a major reason for firms being involved in sponsorship is to establish, strengthen or change their brand image. An example of image transfer to build a brand image is the use of prestigious sports stars, including Cristiano Ronaldo, David Beckham and Rafael Nadal, as models for Armani underwear (Gower 2011). This illustrates what Gwinner and Eaton (1999) refer to as 'meanings'; in that consumers of expensive male underwear have an image of themselves of being as attractive as these sportsmen appear to be; and that the image that these sportsmen have is transferred to the sponsor's product.

Target market specific audiences

A key benefit that sponsorship has over other forms of promotion is that of efficiently and effectively communicating with target market segments. A target market is defined as a group of customers defined by one or more characteristics to which a firm desires to sell their products or services. These characteristics include:

- Demographic – age, gender, ethnic group, religion.
- Socio-economic – see Table 3.3 below for details.
- Psychographic – lifestyle or opinions, interests, hobbies (as an example of psychographics see Table 3.4 below for the family life cycle).
- Geographic – place of residence.

With the exception of marketers of fast moving consumer goods (FMCG) who have a mass market, all marketers segment their market using these characteristics, to facilitate effective and efficient marketing communication.

It is useful to understand that education is usually the most important driver of socio-economic status. The general rule is that the longer a person spends in education, including higher education, the higher their socio-economic status will be. However, these groups are not always a reliable indicator of income as some C1s and C2s can earn considerable amounts if they are self-employed or work in industries such as mining.

Another target market descriptor is their place in the family life cycle, shown in Table 3.4. People's wants, needs and desires change as they progress through the cycle, and this can be an effective and efficient method of describing a target market.

A significant advantage (or benefit) of sponsorship as a marketing communication tool is that it can be more tightly targeted than other media. Mass media such as television, radio and newspapers may have a large proportion of readers/listeners/viewers who do not fall into the marketer's required market segment, whereas the sponsorship of an event can do this. For example, Figure 3.3 shows the audience at a Celine Dion concert, which shows her audience to be in the main, middle aged, white and middle class (SES B and C). Sponsorship of her tour would result in a more effective, tightly targeted campaign for a product that appealed to this target market.

Table 3.3 Classification of socio-economic market segments

Group	Socio-economic group	Occupational examples	Type of events segment is likely to attend	% of population
A	Upper middle class	Professional, higher managerial, university professors.	High cultural events, fund raisers, opera and classical music festivals.	3
B	Middle class	Middle management, university lecturers, journalists, pharmacists, middle-ranking civil servants.	Cultural events (cheaper seats), food and beverage festivals, community festivals, some sporting events.	15
C1	Lower middle class	Supervisors, clerical, junior managerial or administrative, nurses, teachers, sales representatives.	Popular culture events, most sporting events, community festivals.	24
C2	Skilled working class	Builders, fitters, police constables, self-employed tradespersons.	Major sports events, motor vehicle events, community festivals.	28
D	Working class	Semi-skilled and unskilled workers, factory workers, cleaners, drivers.	Some sporting events.	17
E	State benefit reliant	Casual and part-time workers, pensioners.	Free community events.	13

Source: Adapted from Allen *et al.* (2010) and DJS Research (2013).

Table 3.4 Family life cycle

Sequence	Description
First	Bachelor stage: young, single, no ties.
Second	Young married or partnered, no children.
Third	Full nest 1: young married couples with children.
Fourth	Full nest 2: middle-aged married couples with dependent children.
Fifth	Empty nest: older married couples with no resident children, working or retired.
Sixth	Older single people, widowed or divorced, either working or retired.
Variations	Single parents, divorced without dependent children, middle-aged couples without children.

Source: Allen *et al.* (2010).

Figure 3.3 Celine Dion fans
Source: www.celinedion.com/ca/fan-gallery/37

However, even the best marketers can make incorrect decisions about target markets. In 2003 Chrysler decided to be the major sponsor of Dion's *New Day* show and tour. According to *Marketing Vox* (2003), Chrysler was appealing to the wrong target market for their entry vehicle, the product behind the sponsorship, instead of a more up-market auto product, which had more appeal to Celine Dion fans.

So if a marketer's target market had the characteristics of aged 18–35, female, SES of C1 or C2 and in the full nest 1 life stage, then they would simply have to discover an event that had a similar target market and develop a sponsorship programme with the property. Similarly, the property identifies the characteristics of its target market, establishes what products have a similar target market and then constructs a sponsorship plan that can then satisfy the marketing communication objectives of the potential sponsor, enhanced by the fact that the sponsor will be communicating to exactly their target market with little waste – the exemplar of effectiveness.

The principal sponsor of the New Zealand All Blacks rugby team is Adidas, producers and distributors of all kinds of sporting apparel. Their target market – aged 18–45, predominately male, SES A, B and C, resident in New Zealand, with a keen interest in sport, is the same as All Black fans, which makes for tight target marketing. However, Tuttle (2011) explains how marketers sometimes get it wrong, citing how Adidas charged an extraordinarily high price for their All Black jerseys, to which they had sole rights because of their sponsorship.

Media coverage

The next benefit sponsorship can bring a sponsor is that of media coverage of their brand name, which can enhance brand awareness and image. This is usually done by the property offering naming rights to the property in one form or another. The property includes such things as sporting stadia – for example, the Etihad stadia in Melbourne, Australia and Manchester, UK; and sporting teams – for example, competitors in the NASCAR races in the USA all bear their sponsor's names.

Additionally, if the event is televised, as most professional sporting events are, and cultural events usually have a television news presence, the sponsor's brand is shown or mentioned by the commentators. The sponsor's commitment to the event is usually mentioned in the print media, provided the property facilitates this. It is usually done by having all media conferences in a place that have a backdrop with the sponsor's brand clearly shown, or the interviewee wearing an item of clothing with the sponsor's name clearly shown. However, this wearing of logoed caps or other items by sports stars can look artificial and forced and may be detrimental to the image of the sponsor.

This naming right sponsorship also extends to many cultural events – for example, the Man Booker prize. 'The Man Booker Prize promotes the finest in fiction by rewarding the very best book of the year' (Man Booker Prize 2013). The prize is the world's most important literary award and has the power to transform the fortunes of authors and even publishers and is sponsored by the Man Group plc, a 'world leading alternative investment management business' and Booker plc, 'the UK's largest cash and carry operator, offering branded and private-label goods which are sold to over 459,000 customers including independent convenience stores, grocers, leisure outlets, pubs and restaurants within the UK' (Man Booker Prize 2013). This prize is one of the most sought after in the Anglosphere. Every time the prize is mentioned in the media the sponsor's names are also mentioned.

However, this practice can sometimes meet with community dissatisfaction when long established place and team names are removed. The International Olympic Committee, in particular, does not approve of naming rights and all stadia must have a non-commercial name. For example, the Olympic Stadium for the Sydney 2000 Olympics was named Stadium Australia (a most appropriate name in the writer's opinion) but quickly took a sponsor's brand name after the completion of the Games.

Hospitality and entertainment for clients

A benefit that is unique to sponsorship is that of hospitality and entertainment for clients. As Figure 3.2 shows, hospitality enhances loyalty to the product from key client groups such as retailers and wholesalers. As Meenaghan (1983, p. 42) states, 'guest hospitality refers to those opportunities whereby the company can make face-to-face contact with select publics in a prestigious social context, thereby strengthening and personalizing relationships with decision makers, trade channels and business associates'. This gives marketers opportunities to engage in face-to-face marketing communication (personal selling) in an environment that is relaxed, convivial and of some interest to the guest. And of course business can be discussed in a non-threatening atmosphere, where there is little pressure on the customer to agree to a deal. And of course other stakeholders who may have an impact on the firm's operations can also be given hospitality in this way, without breaking any ethical considerations.

As Crompton (1996) points out, hospitality can be extended to important customers and suppliers at events without sponsorship of the event by the use of corporate boxes.

However, if a guest is offered hospitality by a sponsor the experience can be enhanced by the extra stature given to the sponsor, and access to participants and areas unavailable to the general public. The result of this hospitality is that existing significant customers' loyalty to the sponsor's brand is enhanced and reinforced, while other stakeholders' image of the brand is also reinforced.

A contemporary example of this is M&G Investment's (a British investment management company with over 380,000 customers) sponsorship of the Chelsea Flower Show. Their target market would tend to the middle-aged and older, SES AB, empty nesters, who are gardeners or who have an interest in gardening. They are offering a private tour of the M&G garden, guided by the garden's designer, to those who enter a simple competition (RHS 2013) but their sponsorship agreement would also allow them to treat important customers and stakeholders to a tour of the show, followed by suitable food and beverage in congenial surroundings.

Client data base additions

The web site that offers the competition for two tickets to the Chelsea Flower Show (mentioned above) is an excellent example of the next benefit of sponsorship; that of *client data base additions*. Data mining is defined by Linoff and Berry (2011) 'as the process of exploring large amounts of data to establish meaning patterns and rules'. In marketing terms 'data' (a plural word, by the way) is defined as information on consumers' demographics and buying behaviour. However, before data can be mined it must be (a) collected, and (b) meaningful. As M&G Investment's target market is the same as the target market for the Chelsea Flower Show, offering free tickets to their sponsored show enables M&G to gather names, email address and phone numbers of people who are in their target market – meaningful data indeed.

The M&G example is an excellent one of intelligent data collection, but all sponsored events offer similar opportunities, provided some thought goes into the sponsorship deal, which is illustrated by the sponsorship of Australia's biggest football game – the 'State of Origin' rugby league match between New South Wales and Queensland each year. Choosi Insurance is a sponsor, with a link on the game's web site to a simple web site that encourages customers to contact the sponsor (NRL.com 2013). Again there is a match between the target market for the game and the sponsor – males, full nest 1.

It can therefore be seen that opportunities to add to a sponsor's data base of consumer or potential consumers can be an essential element of any sponsorship plan, especially in an age of 'e' and the use of information communication technologies in marketing communications, which make electronic communication both effective and efficient.

Sales promotion

Sales promotion is defined by the American Marketing Association (2012) as 'the media and non-media marketing pressure applied for a predetermined, limited period of time at the level of consumer, retailer, or wholesaler in order to stimulate trial, increase consumer demand, or improve product availability'. In the case of sponsorship, the sponsored event can be used as 'non-media marketing pressure' to stimulate a trial of a product.

An example of this is the sponsorship by Lexus, the prestigious Japanese car maker, of the Lexus Song Quest, part of the New Zealand International Arts Festival held in Wellington, the capital of New Zealand, in 2012 (New Zealand Festival 2013). The Lexus Song Quest, of which Lexus obviously obtained naming rights as part of their sponsorship, is a competition to find the best classical singer in New Zealand. Lexus could offer as a prize for the winner of the Lexus Song Quest a Lexus car, which would stimulate interest and increase brand awareness in its product in its target market – congruent with the target market for the festival – that should lead to increased sales.

Another sponsor of the NZ International Arts Festival is the New Zealand Post Group, a state-owned enterprise that has evolved from being a post office to a bank, a postal service, an express courier service and a web-based promotion service for small businesses. While they probably entered this sponsorship to enhance the brand image of the group, they could use it for sales promotion purposes by devices such as:

- free mail of tickets purchased online (which could also be a way of gathering client data);
- the banking division could offer a fee-free account for all consumers buying more than a designated volume of tickets to the festival;
- tickets required urgently could be sent by their express courier service to consumers.

Any sponsorship plan needs to include whenever possible some form of sales promotion to fully realise its potential.

Product exposure

Events of a particular type are also are suitable for product exposure, as Crompton (1996) points out above, which includes *product experience* and *product sales opportunities*.

For example, a sponsor of MotorExpo, a motor show held in London, New York and Toronto, can offer product trial to potential new customers. If an event of this nature was sponsored by an insurance company, for example, visitors to the show could be offered a discount on car insurance if they purchased an exhibited make within 12 months. Alternatively, a motor oil producer sponsor could give every visitor to the event a sample of their oil to use, with an explanation of its particular virtues. But in fact the sponsor is SMMT, the Society of Motor Manufacturers Traders (SMMT 2013), who are offering product exposure and product experience to all the event's exhibitors.

Agricultural shows such as Sydney's Royal Easter Show are another type of event that offers many product exposure opportunities for sponsor's products. This type of event traditionally has many sponsors in various product categories, mainly because of the many opportunities there are for product experience and product exposure to a target market.

As Crompton (1996) rightly states, it can be a difficult marketing communication task to move consumers from the interest stage to the desire stage. A sponsorship that involves potential consumers being able to either experience or trial a product in an environment that is cost free can be an effective method of doing this.

Sponsorship of an event that involves a mass market, such as the aforementioned agricultural show, or a community fair (e.g. the Yorkshire County Show) offers sales opportunities for sponsor's products in an environment conducive to sales, as well as to use promotional techniques such as giveaways of product samples, sweepstakes or competitions with the product as prizes and the product displayed in an inviting manner.

Conclusion

Event producers are much more likely to attract sponsorship if they see it as a marketing communications tool, based on a much used principle of marketing – the AIDA model and the role of sponsorship in facilitating this, and use this in their proposed benefits to potential sponsors. Marketing managers, by the same token, can establish which sponsorships can most effectively and efficiently fulfil their marketing communication strategies by using the same process. And of course, to maximise the benefits accruing to them from the sponsorship.

Discussion questions

1 Is the addition of R (reinforcement) helpful to understanding the sales funnel? Why? Or why not?
2 How could an automotive insurance company that has newly entered the market use its sponsorship of MotorExpo to get consumers to the action stage of the sales funnel?
3 Rafael Nadal's fee for being the body of Armani is not inconsequential. How could Armani's marketing manager justify this expense to the board?
4 What are some entertainment and hospitality opportunities available to M&G because of their sponsorship of the Chelsea Flower Show? To whom should these be directed?
5 How can KaSperSky improve their sponsorship of the Manly Sea Eagles? Or should they find a different property to sponsor? If so, why?

Vignette: benefits accruing to sponsors of the Olympic Games

The cost of sponsoring an Olympic team or an Olympic Games is substantial. According to the *Economist* (2012) the 11 Top Olympic Sponsors (TOPs) paid a total of US$957 million for the period 2009–12 to be associated with the Olympics in a specific category – Coca-Cola for soft drinks; Panasonic for televisions; Omega for time keeping, etc. These are large sums for any marketing communication budget. What therefore are the benefits that sponsors are hoping to receive for their brand?

The journal *Marketing Magazine* (2012) recently listed what in its opinion were some of the top campaigns using the Olympics, which supplies a useful tool to analyse the benefits the sponsors were trying to receive.

Coca-Cola has been an Olympic partner since 1928 and has used their sponsorship in many different ways. In 1988, for example, their sponsorship of the Calgary Winter Olympics used athletes extolling the virtues of Coke as a social lubricant, which does seem rather unusual in today's social milieu. By 2012 their message was one of connection to sport as they employed Grammy award winning producer Mark Ronson to produce *Move to the Beat*, which incorporated the sounds of five Olympic sports people practising their craft into a catchy tune with lyrics sung by Katy B (Coca-Cola 2012).

Interestingly, Nike has never sponsored an Olympic Games, but was responsible for the first ambush marketing campaign. During the 1996 Atlanta Olympics, Nike used billboard advertising, distributed Nike flags and banners outside stadia and even erected a Nike village near the official athletes' village – a much cheaper exercise than being an official sponsor.

Samsung used the Sydney 2000 Olympics as official wireless communicator partner after having launched the brand in Australia 12 months previously. They produced a special product – the special edition Olympic phone – and played on Australian nationalism as the theme of the accompanying TVC. Their relationship with the Olympics continued to London 2012, which they used to launch their Galaxy S III model.

Another successful example of Olympiad ambush marketing was Qantas' marketing activities surrounding the 2000 Olympics. Even though Ansett (an Australian domestic airline) was the official airline partner, Qantas used the words Olympic in their ads (e.g. 'Australia wide Olympic sale') and Cathy Freeman and other Australian Olympic athletes in their marketing campaigns. The result was that many more Australians thought that Qantas was the official sponsor rather than Ansett. As a result of this the International Olympic Committee tightened the rules regarding the use of the Olympic logo and trademarks to stop this ambush marketing occurring again. Sadly Ansett went bankrupt shortly after the Olympics, with a loss of 20,000 jobs.

McDonalds' sponsorship of the Beijing 2008 Olympics used a theme of people from all over the world coming together in a festival of sport (and eating Big Macs, presumably). However, in China, where there was much pride in China's hosting of the Games, the theme revolved around Chinese success. The slogan they used in China was 'I love it when China wins', which was very successful in the China market, and a useful example of the importance of localisation.

Visa's Go World campaign (Visa 2012) has been used at both summer and winter Olympics since the Beijing 2008 Games, and has recently signed to be a TOP until 2020. Its TVCs feature athletes triumphing against much difficulty, and finish with the words 'More people go with Visa'. They used television, social media, digital, out-of-home (all promotion that reaches the consumer out of their home using media such as billboards, street furniture, buses, etc.) and incentives to connect with fans and potential and existing consumers.

Adidas used a promotional campaign theme of 'Nothing is impossible' that featured sporting stars from various sports and countries describing how they had achieved greatness against adversity. This was adapted to be used in the Chinese market as part of their Beijing 2008 sponsorship to a TVC, online and print campaign featuring a Chinese female basketball player, a male diver and a male footballer with the slogan 'Impossible is nothing', thereby localising their worldwide campaign.

TOP sponsorships require a very large resource investment from these giant international corporations mentioned. What benefits were these corporations endeavouring to receive from this large resource expenditure? How could they evaluate whether this was achieved?

References

Allen, J., McDonnell, I., O'Toole, W. and Harris, R. (2010) *Festival and Special Event Management,* 5th Edition, John Wiley and Sons, Brisbane.

American Marketing Association (2012) *Marketing Power Resource Library*, available at www.marketingpower.com/_layouts/Dictionary.aspx?dLetter=S

Coca-Cola (2012) accessible at www.coca-cola.co.uk/olympic-games/move-to-the-beat-london-2012-mark-ronson.html

Crompton, J. (1996) 'The potential contributions of sports sponsorship in impacting the product adoption process', *Managing Leisure*, vol. 1, no. 4, pp. 199–212.

DJS Research (2013) available at www.djsresearch.co.uk

Economist (2012) 'Sponsor fees reach Olympic proportions', republished in the *Australian Financial Review* available at www.afr.com/p/lifestyle/sport/olympics/sponsor_fees_reach_olympic_proportions_AOXPfqVSelhi7j07I92MLJ 27/07/12

Gower, E. (2011) 'Rafael Nadal in Armani underwear', *Daily Mail*, 21 September, available at http://www.dailymail.co.uk/tvshowbiz/article-2039687/Rafael-Nadal-Armani-underwear-strips-down-new-sizzling-advert.html#ixzz1t79YEDla

Gwinner, K. (1997) 'A model of image creation and image transfer in event sponsorship', *International Marketing Review*, vol. 14, issue 3, pp. 145–158.

Gwinner, K. and Eaton, J. (1999) 'Building brand image through sponsorship: The role of image transfer', *Journal of Advertising*, vol. XXVIII, no. 4, pp. 47–57.

Kotler, P. (1988) *Marketing Management: Analysis, Planning and Control*, Prentice Hall, NJ.

La Martina (2013) available at www.lamartina.com/2010/stores.html

Lavidge, R. and Steiner, G. (1961) 'A model of predictive measurement of advertising effectiveness', *Journal of Marketing*, vol. 25, no. 1, pp. 59–62.

Linoff, G. and Berry, M. (2011) *Data Mining Techniques for Marketing, Sales and Customer Relationship Management*, 3rd edition, Wiley Publishing, Indianapolis.

Man Booker Prize (2013) available at www.themanbookerprize.com/background

Marketing Magazine (2012) 'Top ten Olympic marketing campaigns', 19 April, available at www.marketingmag.com.au/news/top10-olympic-marketing-campaigns-12892/#.UWEbbcrWOg7

Marketing Vox (2003) 'Chrysler campaign fails miserably' accessible at www.marketingvox.com/chrysler_campaign_fails_miserably-014628/

McIlwraith, I. (2012) 'Kia Australia rises up the rankings after learning how to play the game', *Sydney Morning Herald*, 17 January, available at www.smh.com.au/business/kia-australia-rises-up-the-rankings-after-learning-how-to-play-the-game-20120116–1q35j.html#ixzz1sv5YyumY

Meenaghan, J. (1983) 'Commercial sponsorship', *European Journal of Marketing*, vol. 17, issue 7, pp. 5–73.

New Zealand Festival (2013) available at http://festival.co.nz/

NRL.com (2013) available at www.nrl.com/RepGames/StateofOrigin2012/tabid/11131/ Default.aspx

Oh, H. (2002) 'The effect of brand class, brand awareness, and price on customer value and behavioural intentions', *Journal of Hospitality and Tourism Research*, vol. 24, no. 2, May, p. 136.

provenmodels (2013) 'AIDA sales funnel', available at www.provenmodels.com/547/ aida-sales-funnel/

RHS (2013) available at www.mandgchelsea.co.uk/mandg-and-the-rhs.aspx

SMMT (2013) available at www.smmt.co.uk/summi

St Elmo Lewis, E. (1898) 'The AIDA sales funnel model'.

Tuttle, B. (2011) 'Adidas and the All Blacks: How to anger an entire nation of rabid sports fans', *Time: Business and Money*, August, available at http://moneyland.time.com/ 2011/08/25/adidas-the-all-blacks-how-to-anger-an-entire-nation-of-rabid-sports-fans

Visa (2012) *Go World Olympic Marketing Campaign Fact Sheet*, available at http:// corporate.visa.com/_media/olympic-games-media-kit/go-world-background.pdf

Chapter 4

The 'fit' between sponsor and sponsee

Learning outcomes

After reading, discussing and comprehending this chapter, readers will be able to:

- define the meaning of 'fit' in the sponsorship context;
- establish the criteria for fit between a sponsor and a sponsee (the property);
- include the concept of fit in a sponsorship proposal;
- review sponsorship proposals for tightness of fit.

Introduction

The concept of 'fit', or brand/sponsor congruence as it is sometimes called, is of fore-most importance in the use of sponsorship as an integrated marketing communication medium, both for the property and the sponsor. This chapter will firstly define what 'fit' is, and then go on to discuss its ramifications for the sponsorship proposal and implementation. The chapter will also propose a number of tightness-of-fit criteria that can be used to establish just that.

So, what is this thing called fit or congruence? Congruence has a definitive mathematical definition – it occurs when objects are equal in shape and dimension. Fleck and Quester (2007) start their article on this topic by using the old adage of 'birds of a feather flock together', which means that some things fit (or go together) while others are in conflict, and that the ones that do have some unifying characteristic. Identifying those 'fit' characteristics is a fundamental aspect of the marketer's job, and is integral to effective sponsorship activities.

What is 'fit'?

As Fleck and Quester (2007) point out, defining 'fit' or congruence is somewhat problematic because of the vague way the term has been used in the marketing literature. For example 'fit' has been used in the context of brand extensions where an existing brand is extended to incorporate a variation of the existing product. Haig (2011) reports that examples of successful brand extension are Coca-Cola's launch in 1982 of Diet Coke, now one of the biggest selling soft drinks on the globe, and the various brand extensions of the Virgin organisation. However, it is of interest to note that the Coke brand extension into clothing apparel has been nowhere as successful as Diet Coke, and the reason is that there seems little 'fit' between a soft drink and clothing (see Coca-Cola Store 2013).

Haig (2011) goes on to discuss the brand extensions of Virgin – probably the most brand-extended company on the planet. He states that the unifying force behind all these extensions is the persona of Richard Branson, Virgin's chief executive. This enables product types as different as

lifestyle (e.g. Virgin Books, Virgin Active, Virgin Wines);
media and mobile (e.g. Virgin Connect, Virgin Media, Virgin Mobile UK);
money (e.g. Virgin Money Australia, Virgin Money UK, Virgin Giving);
music (e.g. Virgin Festivals, Virgin Megastore);
travel (e.g. Virgin America, Virgin Australia, Virgin Trains)

to be a coherent whole, unified by the personality and charisma of Mr Branson, thereby ensuring 'fit'. However, not all Virgin's extensions were successful, as the miniscule market share of Virgin Cola attests, as well as other forays into wedding dresses, cosmetics, vodka, flowers and others, according to Russell (2012).

Another example of successful brand extension that exemplifies 'fit' is Gillette's extension from razor blades and razors to shaving cream. Consumers associated their razor products with a comfortable shave, which is enhanced by using a complementary shaving cream.

Haig (2011) gives as an exemplar of poor fit the brand extension that Harley Davidson – makers of a well-known American motorbike, which has many thousands of devoted, even passionate followers – undertook. The company attempted to capitalise on this devotion by extending the brand to a wide variety of branded merchandise – T-shirts, socks, cigarette lighters and various motorbike themed ornaments. The real problem for Harley Davidson arose when they used the Harley Davidson name on a range of perfume and aftershave fragrances – a step too far for those passionate Harley devotees. It should have been obvious that there is little 'fit' between an icon of testosterone charged bikers and a Harley branded perfume.

Fleck and Quester (2007, p. 977) quote the work of Heckler and Childers (1992), who conceptualised congruence (or fit) as having two dimensions: relevancy and expectancy. Relevancy is defined as 'degree to which the information contained in the stimulus favours (or hinders) the identification of the theme or message being communicated'. In the Harley example cited above, the information contained in the brand name Harley Davidson hinders identification by potential consumers with an aftershave or perfume product bearing that brand; whereas with the Gillette example, there is a great deal of relevancy as the identification of Gillette shaving cream with the Gillette brand is enhanced by the previous knowledge of the Gillette product.

Expectancy is defined by Heckler and Childers (Fleck and Quester 2007, p. 977) as 'the degree to which an item or information falls into a predetermined schema or a structure evoked by the theme'. In the Harley example, the Harley consumer has a predetermined view, idea, or representation (a schema) of what the Harley Davidson brand means to them. It is somewhat obvious that this schema does not very likely include such products as aftershave and perfume. Whereas existing consumers of Gillette razors would expect that this brand would also produce shaving cream of a high quality.

Therefore it can be seen that these two criteria would be part of any list of tightness-of-fit criteria, and this is discussed further in this chapter.

Other words or phrases used in definitions of congruence in the marketing literature are:

- Boush *et al.* (1987) use *similar* as an essential feature of congruence;
- Boush and Loken (1991) refer to the *typicality* of brand extensions with reference to the similarities it shares with other products sharing the brand name;
- Park *et al.* (1991) introduce *perceived fit*, by which consumers consider if a new product or a brand fits into their perceptions of that brand – for example, if Kellogg introduced a snack food to be consumed at a time other than breakfast, the *perceived fit* may be somewhat tenuous;
- Tauber (1993) uses the word *fit*, which occurs when consumers perceive a new product of a brand to be logical or expected – again the Kellogg analogy is apt;
- Gurhan-Canli and Maheswaran (1998) also use *typicality* to conceptualise the capacity of one product to represent its category – for example, Kellogg's introducing a new type of breakfast cereal would be a 'typical' brand extension – Coco Pops® Chocolatey Liquid Breakfast.

It does appear that the words similar, typicality and perceived fit are used by different marketing scholars to mean the same thing – that is the degree to which the brand extension (or a brand portfolio for that matter) is perceived as similar to the mother brand. In terms of sponsorship therefore, sponsorship fit can be defined as the similarity between the property and the sponsor, which is further expanded in a discussion of congruence below. Congruence simply means suitability or appropriateness of one thing to another; agreement; consistency; and is in this context just a synonym for fit. However, it is much liked in academic circles as it is polysyllabic, and it is used interchangeably with fit in this chapter.

Most concepts of congruence come from the brand extension literature and were first used in this context by Meyers-Levy and Tybout (1989), who defined it as the match between an object and the relevant schema surrounding it, but later Myers-Levy *et al.* (1994) further refined the concept to be the strength of the link between a product and its category. An example of this is the strength of Kellogg in the breakfast cereal category – the company has a strong congruence in this category and would have no difficulty in gaining consumer acceptance by extending its product range in this category.

Another illustration of marketing communication congruence is that of celebrity endorsement. Misra and Beatty (1990) give a definition of this type of congruence that can also be used for sponsorship congruence – occurring when the relevant characteristics of the endorser (the celebrity) are consistent with the relevant attributes of the brand. An apposite example of this is the decision of Nike (the sportswear and sporting goods giant) to use first Tiger Woods and now Rory McIlroy (both of whom are either prior or current golf world number ones) as endorsers of their golfing products. Both celebrities were and are the best in the world at the game of golf and Nike wants to be positioned as the world's best in golf equipment – congruence. However, there is some evidence to suggest that moderate congruence is also conducive to favourable recollections by consumers, especially with repeated exposures (Lane 2000; Sheinin and Schmitt 1994), as is discussed later in the chapter regarding the research done by Fleck and Quester (2007).

Much research had been done on the effectiveness of sponsorship as a marketing communication tool (see, for example, Quester 1997; Quester and Thompson 2001). An oft forgotten point of this type of marketing communications, highlighted by Fleck and Quester (2007) is that the sponsorship is peripheral to the event experience being consumed. That is, consumers first of all attend a sport event, an exhibition or a concert to enjoy that experience, not to absorb a sponsor's message. This may mean that the sponsors face the risk of being ignored, or their message only being superficially received by the consumer. Also, the message is often non-verbal and implicit (use of a logo on a players uniform, for example). It is therefore up to the consumer to understand the message and give it meaning. This means that if the message is incongruent, it stands a good chance of being ignored or not understood in the way the sponsor expected or desired.

That is why much of the academic sponsorship literature has examined the concept of congruence (or 'fit'). Table 4.1 gives pertinent examples of attempts to define 'congruence'.

This trawl through 20 years of academic work on the definition of sponsorship congruence is useful to gain an understanding of the concept and its importance in producing sponsorship activities that are both effective and efficient. Whilst all are helpful, the attempt by Pentecost and Spence (2004) to list the dimensions that ensure 'fit' or congruence between sponsor and property is useful as it can be used to calculate tightness of fit and the criteria to be used in such an exercise.

As well as defining 'fit', much academic research has been done establishing the effect of tightness of fit. These findings are shown in tabular form for ease of comprehension in Table 4.2 below.

Table 4.1 Definition of congruence in the academic sponsorship literature

Source	Definition
Otker and Hayes 1988	*Link* between sponsor and event on a continuum from very weak to very strong.
McDonald 1991	*Direct relevancy* when sponsor's product can be used in the event.
	Indirect relevancy when some aspects of the sponsor relate to the event.
D'Astous and Bitz 1995	*Link* between sponsor and property.
Gwinner 1997	*Similarity* based *on functional aspect*, when the brand is used by event participants.
	Similarity based on *image*, when the image of the event is linked to the image of the brand.
Didellon 1997	*Perceived alignment*: overall positive judgement of the logical connection between sponsor and property.
McDaniel 1999	*Match-up* between sponsor and event: perceived similarity between sponsor attributes and event attributes.
Johar and Pham 1999	*Relatedness*: existence of a semantic link between sponsor and event.
Speed and Thompson 2000	*Fit or congruence*: attitude toward the pair sponsor/event and the degree to which the pair is perceived as well matched.
Becker-Olsen and Simmons 2002	*Native fit*: degree to which the sponsor and the cause can be deemed to go well together, regardless of any communication.
	Created fit: fit induced by communication and not intrinsic to the organisations involved.
Basil and Basil 2003	*Fit*: complementary association.
	Complementarity: characteristic of two entities with shared goal and objectives.
Rodgers 2004	*Relevancy*: natural proximity between the sponsor's products and the sponsored objects.
Louis 2004	*Similarity*: degree to which individuals (event consumers) perceive that the association between the sponsor and the property is logical or not.
Pentecost and Spence 2004	*Fit*: made up of six dimensions – target markets, image, location, typicality, clash, complementarity.

Source: Adapted from Fleck and Quester 2007.

Table 4.2 The effects of congruence on sponsorship

Author	Findings
Otker and Hayes 1988	Suggested that sponsors benefit from a greater impact in terms of image enhancement if sponsor and event are congruent.
D'Astous and Bitz 1995	There is a non-linear relationship between sponsor/property congruence and the perceived image of the sponsor, such that the sponsor's image improves when congruence grows from weak to moderate but not when congruence grows from moderate to strong.
Gwinner 1997	Suggests that congruence induces stronger associations between sponsor and property and enhances image transfer.
Didellon 1997	Transfers between events and sponsors, be they cognitive of affective in nature, occur with the same effectiveness, whether congruence is moderate or strong.
McDaniel 1999	Congruence positively influences attitudes towards advertising/sponsorship (and the more congruent the more positive the attitude) but it has no effect on attitude towards the brand or purchase intentions.
Johar and Pham 1999	Congruence between sponsor and property enhances sponsor recall. Product category dominance also plays a part.
Gwinner and Eaton 1999	Congruence between sponsor and property (be it functional or image based) enhances image transfer (cognitive or affective).
Speed and Thompson 2000	Congruence between sponsor and property improves sponsorship effectiveness – i.e., interest in sponsor, attitudes to sponsor and purchase intentions.
	Congruence is a moderating variable in relation to consumer response to sponsorship. The stronger the congruence, the greater the impact of interest in the event, and the weaker the congruence, the greater the impact of importance of the event.
Jagre et al. 2001	Not formally tested but suggest that weaker congruence induced a higher level of recall than moderate or high level of congruence. However, weak congruence induces less favourable attitude than either moderate of high levels of congruence.
Becker-Olson and Simmons 2002	Low levels of congruence reduce the sponsors' equity in terms of favourable attitudes and beliefs when compared to no sponsorship, whereas a high level of congruence increases sponsors' equity. Attitude towards sponsorship and positioning act as a mediating variables for the effects of congruence (be it created or spontaneous).
Basil and Basil 2003	Congruence, even weak, has positive effects on purchase intentions and attitudes.

(*Continued*)

Table 4.2 Continued

Author	Findings
Rodgers 2004	Congruence between sponsor and event enhances sponsor recall, attitudes towards sponsor and purchase intention. Event credibility is a moderating variable. The greater the event credibility, the positive the perceptions of a congruent sponsor.
Rifon *et al.* 2004	Congruence between sponsor and cause generates greater attribution of altruistic motives to the sponsor, higher levels of credibility and more positive attitudes. Altruistic motives are mediating variables of the relationship between congruence and credibility. Sponsor credibility mediates the relationship between perceived motives and attitudes towards the sponsor.
Louis 2004	Congruence is associated with stronger affective transfer between sponsor and property.
Fleck and Quester 2007	Sponsorship congruence is derived from two distinct sources, expectancy and relevancy. Moderate levels of congruence are more effective than high or low levels.

Source: adapted from Fleck and Quester 2007.

This review of 20 years of research reveals that the great majority of research findings regarding 'fit' or congruence show it to be an essential ingredient of any effective sponsorship. However, a few researchers found that moderate levels of congruence can be more effective than high or low levels.

This can be explained by the findings of Fleck and Quester (2007) that congruence comes from two variables – expectancy and relevancy. As discussed previously, they define expectancy as relating to a predetermined image of the sponsor, and relevancy as occurring when the sponsor/property relationship makes sense and contributes clearly some meaning to the sponsor. As previously mentioned, sponsorship is peripheral to a consumer's enjoyment of the event experience. A degree of unexpectedness can therefore enhance a sponsorship's effectiveness, while at the same time the sponsor's product manifests some relevance to the property.

The example quoted by Fleck and Quester (2007) to illustrate their concept of the two variables that make for congruency – relevancy and expectancy – is a pharmaceutical company that makes cough lozenges sponsoring musical performances at the Sydney Opera House. Though at first glance the fit between a classical music performance and cough lozenges seems somewhat remote, nothing is more annoying to a concert goer than coughing fits from fellow patrons. Therefore, though the expectancy may take some time to sink into the consciousness of the consumer, when it does both the expectancy and relevancy of the sponsorship to the consumer is enhanced.

The point that Fleck and Quester (2007) make is that while the more consumers who see the relationship between sponsor and property as matched, the more effective is the sponsorship, it is conceivable that a certain degree of incongruence (e.g. in the instance described in the previous paragraph) may enhance consumers' response to a sponsorship, provided it is perceived as interesting and positive. This view was shared by D'Astous and Bitz (1995) and Jagre *et al.* (2001), whose research concluded that a moderately inconsistent match enhances consumer perceptions of the sponsor.

In summing up, it is clear that the academic research shows that congruence or fit between the sponsor and the event property has many positive outcomes, including:

- greater image enhancement;
- induces stronger associations between event and sponsor;
- positively influences attitudes towards the sponsor;
- enhanced image transfer;
- improves sponsorship effectiveness; i.e. interest in and attitude to sponsor and increased sales;
- has positive effects on purchase intentions, even when weak;
- enhances sponsor recall, attitudes to sponsor and purchase intention;
- generates greater attribution of altruistic motives to the sponsor;
- stronger affective transfer between property and sponsor.

However, when used in an innovative and interesting way, a moderate to low level of congruence may work to make the sponsorship effective as long as relevancy is maintained.

Criteria for fit

Now that it has been established what 'fit' is, it is time to establish the criteria for effective 'fit'. Fleck and Quester (2007) argue that expectancy and relevancy are the two most important criteria for effective fit, but Pentecost and Spence's (2004) multi-dimensional criteria also comprise a useful tool for establishing tightness of fit. Each is discussed in turn.

Expectancy

The concept comes from marketing theory and means a type of consumer attitude theory stating that consumers rank products based on the total of their characteristics. It can be conceptualised thus:

Palmgreen (1984) described how a consumer's expectations are formed: from their intrinsic beliefs, their evaluations of how various prodcts can gratify a need, and from the media messages consumed. Their evaluation of the product and its ability to gratify their need then reinforces or not their expectations of the product.

What Fleck and Quester (2007) argue is that a sponsor/property relationship is expected if it relates to a predetermined sponsor schema. In other words does the sponsorship meet the consumers' expectations about the behaviour of the sponsor? For example, McDonalds, a major sponsor of various events, would not be expected to sponsor the 2013 Open Golf Championship (Great Britain), and if they did so, certainly would not meet the expectancy criteria. It is of interest to note that the Open Championship does not describe their sponsors as such, but as patrons (The Open Championship 2013). The only 'patron' that does not meet the expectancy criteria is a Korean industrial company, Doosan, an 'ISB (Infrastructure Support Business) provider, specializing in power generation, seawater desalination, construction & engineering, heavy machinery & construction equipment, energy, national defence and production facilities' (Doosan 2013). The reasoning behind Doosan's marketing expenditure on its sponsorship of the Open Championship can only be guessed at.

Relevancy

Relevancy is when the sponsorship makes sense and contributes some meaning to the sponsor. Using again the 2013 Open Championship example, 'patrons' such as Rolex, Mercedes Benz, HSBC, Ralph Lauren and MasterCard would meet the criteria of relevance as these are all high-end products that appeal to the consumers of arguably golf's most prestigious competition. However, it is difficult to establish the relevancy in NTT Data's 'patronage' of this event. However, televised golf, like most sports, is now a high-tech exercise that uses a great deal of information communication technology (ICT), and perhaps like the cough lozenges, this sponsorship will prove to be effective and efficient for NTT Data.

Fleck and Quester's (2007) research did establish that using expectancy and relevancy as the source for congruence or fit is valid, and – as their research was conducted in Europe and Australia – is valid across cultures. The conclusions from their research were that the intrinsically peripheral nature of event sponsorship 'requires that they stand out in consumers' perception, something only a degree of unexpectedness or surprise can achieve' (Fleck and Quester 2007, p. 993). However, the sponsorship must also exhibit some degree of relevancy or the association between sponsor and property is meaningless and fails to impinge on consumers' consciousness. This therefore would be the rationale for NTT Data's sponsorship of the Open Championship, as it has relevancy (use of ICTs in distribution of data) coupled with a certain degree of unexpectedness.

Dimensions of fit

Pentecost and Spence's (2004) research into fit using semi-structured interviews with sponsorship managers concluded that there are six dimensions to fit, namely target markets, image, geography, typicality, complementarity and clash. Each is discussed in turn and examples given.

Target market

This is so obvious that it beggars belief that sponsors can sponsor events that are not consumed by the market for their products. McDonald's for example is one of the largest investors in sponsorship as a marketing communication tool, but they would never be a sponsor of the Open Championship as their target market is not at all interested in competitive golf. It is of interest to note that one of the questions McDonald's ask events or causes seeking sponsorship is 'Profile of the target audience'. They know that the first criterion of fit is congruent target markets.

However, six of the eight 'patrons' of the Open Championship do have congruent markets with golf fans – predominantly male; over 40; socio-economic status (SES) A or B; relatively affluent – HSBC, Nikon, Ralph Lauren, Mercedes Benz, MasterCard, Rolex. It is this ability to match target markets that can make sponsorship a very effective and efficient marketing communication medium. In other words their message is being sent to exactly those the sponsor wants to receive it, with no wastage. Compare this with advertising in a newspaper or a television programme where the message is either ignored by the target market or wasted on those who fall outside the target. Expectancy theory (or better in this case, unexpected theory) can be the reason why the other two sponsors of the property are involved.

Image

This concerns the mental picture a consumer has of a product and an event, both real and perceived. Brand image is developed over time by consumers' experience with a product and by all the marketing communications that a consumer has received about a product. McDonald's has an image with most consumers of a fast food colossus that delivers cheap food quickly and efficiently. By contrast the image of the Open Championship is that of a high quality, well-run sporting competition that combines history, tradition and skill that is followed with interest by millions of affluent golfers around the globe. It is therefore obvious that there is an image clash, and McDonald's would be wasting their marketing funds sponsoring the Open. However, the image of a brand such as Ralph Lauren and the image of the Open Championship are congruent, which makes for effective integrated marketing sponsorship activity.

Geography

This refers to localising a sponsorship so it appeals to local sentiment rather than just a standard nation-wide message. Sheep Day in Skipton, North Yorkshire, is very much a local community event whose sponsorship would be an ideal marketing communication medium for a local business, for example, the Yorkshire Bank; the event also has other advantages of fit – an event with a very local Yorkshire image and a congruent target market.

The other aspect of geographic fit worth considering is that a sponsorship message that works well in one area may need some tweaking for it to work as well in a different location. For example, Coca-Cola's (another large sponsor of many community events) sponsorship messages would vary depending on the location.

Typicality

Typicality means the capacity to match the attributes of a sponsor's product with characteristics of the event. In other words consumers would find a resemblance between the sponsor's brand or product and an event's characteristics. For example, beer is a typical drink consumed by many followers of football, which means there is a fit between the two. Another example of typicality is Swisse Men's Multivite (a multivitamin supplement) sponsorship of Australian cricket. A product designed to 'support energy, stamina and vitality' (Cricket Australia 2013)) matches characteristics of a successful sportsman (or someone hoping to be successful).

Alternatively, lack of typicality can be a contributor to a congruence mismatch. An example is Jayco's (Australia's largest manufacturer of caravans and camping products) sponsorship of Cycling Australia (Australia's professional cycling organisation). At first glance there seems little typicality between professional cycling and recreational caravanning and camping, though Jayco's marketing director does claim that the two are an ideal fit (DPPR 2013).

Complementarity

This deals with the perceived fit between sponsors. It is apparent that six of the eight sponsors of the Open Championship 2013 have a complementary relationship. That is, they are in different product categories, but have the same quality, exclusive and stylish image that matches the image of the event property. This complementarity can leverage the individual sponsorship by association. Doosan and NTT Data are not complementary to the other sponsors, but are probably engaging in this sponsorship to improve their brand recognition in a particular international demographic.

Clash

Clash is the opposite of sponsor complementarity, in which two or more sponsors are from the same product category. It is a cardinal rule of sponsorship that there can only be one sponsor from each product category, to avoid a clash of messages. This becomes problematic when an individual player is sponsored by one product and the competition in which the player is involved is sponsored by a competing product.

Additionally, the use of controversial sponsors has been researched by Ruth and Simonin (2003), who concluded that a sponsorship by 'stigmatised' sponsors – tobacco, alcohol, gambling, products or firms with a tarnished image, for example – can 'work against positive evaluation of an event' (p. 26). However, many of these sponsors may be prepared to pay a higher price for their sponsorship, provided there is no legal restriction on their participation. It then becomes a judgement of the event's marketing director whether to gain extra sponsorship revenue at the risk of alienating their event consumers.

Conclusion: fit in a sponsorship proposal

It has been shown that fit or congruence (in this context the words are interchangeable, but fit is preferred as it is one syllable rather than three) is an integral part of effective and efficient sponsorship activities. Any event property, from the smallest community event to a major community or cultural event, must ensure that any pitches for sponsorship are to organisations that fit their event, using the criteria laid out in this chapter. In the same way, marketers seeking to use sponsorship of events as an integrated marketing communication medium to communicate with their target market must also ensure there is a fit between their product, its image, its market demographics and the property's image and target market.

Without a tight fit between sponsor/property, the effectiveness and efficiency of the sponsorship activity can be greatly diminished, with the integrated marketing communications of the sponsor's brand falling on deaf or unopened ears.

Sponsorship fit vignette: Qantas and the Australian Grand Prix

Qantas is Australia's major international and domestic airline and is one of the world's leading airlines. It has an image, carefully constructed over many years, of being technologically advanced, international in outlook, providing quality service in innovative and satisfying ways, reliable and safe.

The Formula One single seat racing car circuit consists of 20 races starting with the Melbourne Grand Prix – the races are known as Grands Prix – in March and finishing with the *Grand Premo do Brasil* in November (Formula 1 2012). Races are held in Asia, Europe, Australia and the Americas. The contestants are international in origin, as are the cars and technology used in the races. The 2010 Melbourne race drew 40 million viewers from around the world.

The Formula One circuit (the 'formula' is a set of rules that must be followed by entrants) is followed by very large number of people, mainly men, around the world, and is therefore suitable for a brand with an international reach.

Qantas was the naming rights sponsor in 1997–2001 and 2010–2012, but has been one of the sponsorship partners since its commencement in Australia in 1985. An examination of the criteria for a tight sponsorship fit shows that Qantas has this fit with the Australian Grand Prix.

Target market These are congruent as followers of Formula One racing are largely men, aged 22–45 who are better educated and earn more than the average person in their country (F1 2012) – a Qantas target market

Image Qantas' image described above is congruent with that of Formula One – high-tech; international; high quality; the world's best in their field.

Geography As Qantas is an international brand, it is pertinent that the event they sponsor has an international television audience of 40 million, which means that there is no waste in the audience for their messages.

Typicality A Formula One Grand Prix event has characteristics of internationalism, worldwide sourcing of drivers and entrants, excitement and technological advances, which means that a brand like Qantas has many common characteristics.

Complementarity This event has 48 sponsors ranging from Mercedes Benz (very complementary for Qantas) to Spotless, a dry-cleaning company, that is perhaps not so complementary. However, Qantas is the only sponsor in the transport category, and some of the other sponsors share their quality image.

Clash There are no clashes with other sponsoring brands, as Qantas is the sole sponsor in the transport category and none of the other 47 sponsors are controversial in any way. It can therefore be seen that there is a tight fit between the event and the sponsor. The only variable is the price, and Qantas has obviously thought the price to high because they have relinquished their naming rights to Rolex.

There have been eight naming rights sponsors of the event since its inauguration in 1985 – some have tighter fit than others. For example, Fosters, a well-known beer brand, was naming rights sponsor from 1986 to 1993 and from 2002 to 2006. It is difficult to see how an alcoholic drink is congruent with driving cars very fast.

Discussion questions

1 Define 'fit' in your own words.
2 What is the difference between fit and congruence?
3 Give an example with which you are familiar of sponsorship fit and another which has a lack of fit.

4   Give reasons for your answers to question 3.
5   The other naming sponsors of the Australian Formula One Grand Prix are:

Mitsubishi (Japanese car manufacturer);
EDS (American IT company);
Transurban (a toll road owner and operator with interests in Australia and the
     United States);
ING (a Dutch insurance company);
Rolex (a Swiss watch company).
                              (http://en.wikipedia.org/wiki/Australian_Grand_Prix)

Using a 1–10 scale, rate the tightness of fit for each of these sponsors, with
reasons.

References

Basil, D. and Basil, M. (2003) 'Towards an understanding of fit: Effects of association
    and complementarity in cause-related marketing alliances', *Proceedings of the 30th
    International Research Seminar in Marketing*, La Londe-Les-Maures, France pp.
    161–173.
Boush, D. and Loken, B. (1991) 'A process-tracing study of brand extension evaluation',
    Journal of Marketing Research, vol. 28, pp. 16–28.
Boush, D., Shipp, S., Loken, B., Gencturk, E., Crockett, S., Kennedy, E., Minshall, B.,
    Misurell, D., Rochford, L. and Strobel, J. (1987) 'Affect generalisation to similar and
    dissimilar brand extensions', *Psychology and Marketing*, vol. 4, pp. 225–237.
Coca-Cola Store (2013) accessible at www.coca-colastore.com/products/cocacola_
    apparel/womens_apparel)
Cricket Australia (2013) available at www.cricket.com.au/
D'Astous, A. and Bitz, P. (1995) 'Consumer evaluations of sponsorship programmes',
    European Journal of Marketing, vol. 29, no. 12, pp. 6–22.
Doosan (2013) accessible at www.doosan.com/en/brand/story.jsp
DPPR (2013) available at www.drpr.com.au/public-relations-blog/2010/10/07/sponsorship-
    has-to-be-the-right-fit/
F1 (2012) available at www.f1deals.com/blog/demographics-spectators-formula-grand-
    prix.html
Fleck, N. and Quester, P. (2007) 'Birds of a feather flock together . . . definition, role
    and measure of congruence: An application to sponsorship', *Psychology and
    Marketing*, vol. 24, no. 11, pp. 975–1000.
Formula 1 (2013) available at www.formula1.com/races/calendar.html
Gurhan-Canli, Z. and Maheswaran, D. (1998) 'The effects of extensions on brand name
    dilution and enhancement', *Journal of Marketing Research*, vol. 18, pp. 464–473.
Gwinner, K. (1997) 'A model of image creation and image transfer in event sponsor-
    ship', *Journal of Marketing Research*, vol. 18, pp. 39–50.
Haig, M. (2011) *The Truth About the 100 Biggest Branding Mistakes of All Time*, Kogan
    Page, London.
Heckler, S. and Childers, T. (1992) 'The role of expectancy and relevancy in memory for

verbal and visual information: What is incongruency?' *Journal of Consumer Research*, vol. 18, pp. 475–492.

Jagre, E., Watson, J. and Watson, J. (2001) 'Sponsorship and congruity theory: A theoretical framework for explaining consumer attitude and recall of event sponsorship', *NA–Advances in Consumer Research*, vol. 28, ed. Gilly, M. C. and Meyers-Levy J., Association for Consumer Research, Valdosta, GA, pp. 439–445.

Lane, V. (2000) 'The impact of ad repetition and ad content on consumer perceptions of incongruent extensions', *Journal of Marketing*, vol. 64, pp. 80–91.

Meyers-Levy, J., Louie, T. and Curren, M. (1994) 'How does the congruity of brand names affect evaluations of brand name extensions?' *Journal of Applied Psychology*, vol. 79, pp. 46–53.

Meyers-Levy, J. and Tybout, A. (1989) 'Schema congruity as a basis for product evaluation', *Journal of Consumer Research*, vol. 16, pp. 39–54.

Misra, S. and Beatty, S. (1990) 'Celebrity spokesperson and brand congruence: An assessment of recall and affect', *Journal of Business Research*, vol. 21, pp. 159–173.

Palmgreen, P. (1984) 'Uses and gratifications: A theoretical perspective', in Bostrom, R. (ed.), *Communication Yearbook*, vol. 8, Sage, Beverley Hills, CA, pp. 20–55.

Park, C., Milberg, S. and Lawson, R. (1991) 'Evaluation of brand extensions: The role of product feature similarity and brand concept consistency', *Journal of Consumer Research*, vol. 18, pp. 185–193.

Pentecost, R. and Spence, M. (2004) 'Exploring the dimensions of fit within sports sponsorship', *Conference Proceedings ANZMAC Wellington*, available at http://pandora. nla.gov.au / pan / 25410 / 20050805–0000 / 130.195.95.71_8081 / WWW/ANZMAC2004 / CDsite/authors.html

Quester, P. (1997) 'Awareness as a measure of sponsorship effectiveness: The Adelaide Formula One Grand Prix and evidence of incidental ambush effects', *Journal of Marketing Communications*, vol. 3, pp. 1–20.

Quester, P. and Thompson, B. (2001) 'Advertising and promotion leverage on arts sponsorship effectiveness', *Journal of Advertising Research*, vol. 41, pp. 33–47.

Rifon, N. J., Choi, S. M., Trimble, C. S. and Li, H. (2004) 'Congruence effects in sponsorship', *Journal of Advertising*, vol. 33, no. 1, pp. 29–42.

Russell, M. (2012) 'Richard Branson's fails: 14 Virgin companies that went bust', *Business Insider*, April, available at www.businessinsider.com/richard-branson-fails-virgin-companies-that-went-bust-2012–4?op=1#ixzz2DU7BiGfF

Ruth, J., and Simonin, B. (2003) 'Brought to you by brand A and brand B', *Journal of Advertising*, vol. 32, no. 3, pp. 19–30.

Sheinin, D. and Schmitt, B. (1994) 'Extending brands with new product concepts: The role of category attribute congruity, brand affect, and brand breadth', *Journal of Marketing Research*, vol. 31, pp. 30–42.

The Open Championship (2013) available at www.theopen.com

Chapter 5

Integrated marketing communication

Learning outcomes

After reading and discussing the contents of this chapter, students will be able to:

- define and describe integrated marketing communication (IMC);
- show an understanding of how IMC has evolved and the levels of integration;
- outline reasons for the growth in the IMC approach and how sponsorship fits.

Introduction

Integrated marketing communication (IMC) is the term applied to the concept that all forms of communication and messaging are carefully linked together.

At its most basic level, IMC means integrating all the marketing tools, so that they work together in harmony.

Here is more detailed explanation (Moore 1992, p. 1):

> IMC is the strategic co-ordination of multiple communication voices. Its aim is to optimise the impact of persuasive communication on both consumer and non-consumer (e.g. trade, professional) audiences by co-ordinating such elements of the marketing mix as advertising, public relations, promotions, direct marketing and package design.

While sponsorship is not included in Moor's examples of the marketing mix, it could easily be listed as one of these elements.

Marketing tools work more effectively if they work together in harmony rather than in isolation. The outcome is greater than it would be if the marketing tools were not used to speak consistently with one voice all the time.

Background

Before we explore IMC in more detail here is a bit of background (Holm 2006). IMC became a hot topic in 1990s in the field of marketing. Four stages of IMC have been identified, starting from tactical co-ordination to financial and strategic integration. Holm's (2006) research suggests that the majority of firms have not progressed beyond the first stages and very few have moved to a strategic level. In fact Kitchen (1997) stated that IMC 'is progressing into acceptability and is becoming entrenched as perceived "academic wisdom" in general marketing'.

Commercial enterprises constantly look for efficiencies, and for ways they can increase productivity and decrease costs; IMC theoretically provides a centralised platform for linkage of content for focusing the message.

Levels of integration

Beyond the basic communications tools, IMC has the potential to impact other layers and business operations. These include horizontal, vertical, internal, external and data integration.

Horizontal integration occurs across business functions – for example, production, finance, distribution and communications working together and aware that their decisions and actions send messages to customers.

Vertical integration means that marketing and communications objectives must support the higher level corporate objectives and missions.

Meanwhile *internal integration* requires internal marketing – ensuring all staff are informed and motivated about any new developments from new campaigns to new corporate identities, new service standards, new strategic partners and so on.

External integration requires service providers from outside the organisation such as design agencies and public relations agencies to work collaboratively to deliver an integrated message. This is where sponsorship and where the brand and property fit in strategic alignment with the client and their IMC.

Data integration refers to a centralised information system across an organisation. In fact the Customer Relationship Management (CRM) role has become one of the more recent marketing focuses, providing extensive records for businesses and their ways to build loyalty and long-term relationships with customers. It is easier and more cost effective to keep a customer than to win a new customer.

Benefits of IMC

While IMC requires significant effort, it delivers many benefits. It can save money, time and stress; it can create competitive advantage and can lead to increases in sales and profits.

IMC focuses the communications around customers and assists them in moving through the various stages of the buying process. The organisation simultaneously consolidates its image, develops a dialogue and nurtures its relationship with customers.

This Customer Relationship Management (CRM) cements a bond of loyalty with customers which can protect them from the inevitable onslaught of competition. The aim to keep a customer for life is a powerful competitive advantage.

IMC also increases profits through efficiencies and cost savings. At its most basic level, a unified message has more impact than disconnected messages. In a busy world, a consistent, consolidated and crystal clear message has a better chance of cutting through the 'noise' of the seemingly endless messages which bombard customers every day.

In addition to this, brand equity (Sreedhar Madhavaram 2005) can be significantly enhanced through the use of integrated marketing by ensuring consistency of message, design and identity. Brand equity is the marketing effects and outcomes that accrue to a branded product compared with those that would accrue to an identical product with an unbranded name: for example, an unbranded cola drink compared with Coca-Cola.

Initial research suggests that images shared in advertising and direct mail boost both advertising awareness and mail-out responses. Indeed it has been shown that a strategic consistency-based integration strategy has more positive effects on information processing, attitude and recall of a communication campaign compared to a non-integration strategy (Angeles Navarro 2006).

Carefully linked messages also assist customers by providing reminders, updates and special offers which, in a systematic way, help them move through the stages of their buying process.

Communications that are not integrated send disconnected messages which reduce the impact of the message. This may also confuse and frustrate customers. On the other hand, integrated communications present a reassuring sense of order.

Consistent images and relevant, useful, messages help nurture long-term relationships with customers. Customer data bases can identify which customers need what information when following or reading their whole buying life.

IMC reduces costs by minimising expenses such as graphics and photography since they can be shared and used across various platforms such as online, print advertising and brochures. Indeed (Taylor 2010), co-ordination of all communications and points with the consumer is very valuable in creating a proactive rather than reactive work environment.

Sponsorship and IMC

Sponsorship as a marketing communications tool is different from traditional media because it attempts to persuade consumers indirectly rather than directly as with press, radio and televison advertising (Kelly and Whiteman 2010).

Sponsorship of the event or property must nevertheless be consistent with the overall brand or product strategy of the sponsor. Grohs (2004) agrees the event sponsor's fit is increasing positive consumer behaviour and awareness. It has also been found (Speed and Thompson 2000) that the use of advertising and promotion, often referred to as leveraging, in conjunction with sponsorship, can significantly differentiate a brand from its competitors and that one benefit sponsorship has over advertising is that although advertising can change a consumer's perception of a specific product, sponsorship can change the perception of a specific sponsor and all the brands falling under it.

Overall Walliser's (2003, p. 9) international review of sponsorship states 'sponsorship today seems legitimised as a versatile, multifunctional communication tool whose benefit is greatest when used as one element in an integrated communications strategy'.

Social media and impact on IMC

The advent of social media provides challenges and opportunities for IMC. Most previous tools of IMC were one-way and sent messages outwards with little or no opportunity for incoming messages such as print, television and radio advertising, public relations, sponsorship, etc. The process was therefore able to be controlled and contained. Social media changed this.

It was Faulds (2009) who found that the content, timing and frequency of social media-based conversations occuring between consumers are outside the manager's direct control. As a result managers need to shape consumer discussions in a manner that is consistent with the IMC message. This includes providing consumers with networking platforms and using blogs and other social media tools and other IMC channels.

Barriers to IMC

Despite its many benefits IMC also has many barriers.

On top of the usual reluctance to change and the challenges of communicating with a wide variety of target audiences, there are many other hurdles which restrict IMC. These include: business unit isolation; compromised creativity; time conflicts; and a lack of management vision and risk taking. These findings are backed up by Kitchen (2005), who suggests that the early promise of IMC has been fading as organisations are not taking the philosophy of IMC seriously even when faced with the prospect of constant efficiencies.

For example, there is business unit isolation: this may be the outcome of physical location or a particular management style on the part of managers who are protective in relation to their budgets and power base.

In fact some organisational structures isolate communications, data, and even managers from each other. Concerns about customer's personal information and its potential misuse in breaching privacy build barriers can inhibit IMC. Structurally too IMC can be hindered. For example, the public relations function often does not report to marketing but to the CEO; similarly, the sales force rarely meets the advertising department.

It might also be the case that by embracing IMC the organisation ends up aligning itself with a message that may be seen to be hypocritical – an airline promoting its safety record just before a plane crash or, a global FMCG company promoting sustainability while undertaking massive sampling campaigns that involve substantial packaging and waste.

Even if such activities are not hypocritical, they may not be fitting. Kelly and Whiteman (2010, pp. 28–9) found that the success of a sponsorship relied on:

- consumer perceived fit between the sponsor and the event or property;
- consumer personal relevance and liking for an event or property;
- sponsorship leverage through the integration of other marketing communication tools.

While the client is the client and the particular origin of the creative idea should not matter, it does. An advertising agency will be less enthusiastic about developing a creative idea generated by, say, an activations agency, preferring to develop their own.

IMC can compromise creativity. Rather than being a matter of 'look at me', slightly crazy promotions all have to fit within the IMC framework. The joy of out-of-control creativity may be compromised, but the creative challenge may be greater and ultimately more satisfying when operating within a tighter, and more integrated, creative brief.

The addition of time scales into a creative brief provides further barriers to IMC. Some material that is developed will be for the long term while other material will be for shorter-term advertising or sales promotions designed to boost quarterly sales. Nevertheless these objectives do not conflict and should be accommodated within a properly planned IMC.

Planning like this is not common. A survey in 1995 (Kitchen 1997) revealed that most managers lack expertise in IMC. The research indicates that it is not just managers, but also agencies that lack expertise. This in part is due to a proliferation of single discipline agencies. The result being that there is a limited number of people experienced in all the marketing communications disciplines. This lack of knowledge is then compounded by a lack of commitment.

Looking at IMC from the perspective of the property rather than the sponsor is very useful and can be a very beneficial way to market events. Prakash Vel (2010) found that a world music festival launch in Dubai in 2009 recorded five times its budget target of visitors, 89 per cent satisfaction and a staggering 99 per cent of visitors stating that they would return. One of the findings is that IMC can lead to a change in the marketing mix; in this case it led to increased use of social media to reach its audience.

Communications theory

IMC is informed by communications theory. This examines the process of communication and the manner in which people communicate and process information. There are a number of different models of communication theory. The simplest model shows a sender sending a message to a receiver who receives and understands it. Unfortunately this model does not replicate reality, as messages are misunderstood, simply ignored or never reach their destination.

Detailed understanding of the needs, emotions, interests and activities of the customer is essential to ensure the accuracy and relevance of any message.

Instead of 'noisy' advertisements encouraging immediate purchase or hard sell, many messages are often created or 'encoded' so that the hard sell becomes a more subtle soft sell. The sender creates or encodes the message in a form that can be easily understood or decoded by the receiver.

Clever encoding also helps a message to cut through the clutter. If the audience spots the message and then decodes or interprets it correctly the message is successful. The marketer then looks for 'feedback' such as coupons returned from mail-outs, likes on Facebook or clicks to web sites, to see if the audience has decoded the message correctly.

Alongside the single step model there are many others. Sponsorship is one of these channels, as would be messages received indirectly through a friend's recommendation. This is referred to as multi-channel communication.

Understanding how multi-phase communications works helps marketers communicate through the various channels – mass communications and individual endorsements that target opinion leaders, events and property owners and other influential people.

The manner in which messages are selected and processed in the minds of the target market is a complex question. Although it is over 70 years old, rather simplistic and too hierarchical, a message model such as AIDA attempts to map the mental processes through which a buyer passes en route to making a purchase.

Attention, Interest, Desire and Action – AIDA

AIDA is an acronym for a marketing process that describes a series of events that may be undergone when a person is selling a product or service.

- A – Attention (Awareness): attract the attention of the customer.
- I – Interest: raise customer interest by focusing on and demonstrating advantages and benefits (instead of focusing on features, as in traditional advertising).
- D – Desire: convince customers that they want and desire the product or service and that it will satisfy their needs.
- A – Action: lead customers towards taking action and/or purchasing.

Using a system like this gives one a general understanding of the psychological process of marketing leading to sales.

The AIDA model (Figure 5.1) was first introduced in 1898 by St Elmo Lewis, an advertising and sales executive. It has been accepted for many years that the strike rate of sales or behaviour change is a proportion of the total number approached. For example, a television advertising campaign reaches a large audience knowing that only a few will buy. Therefore it is accepted that there will be significant wastage.

Despite significant advances in the intervening years, many advertising and marketing decisions today remain based on the AIDA model (Cleary 2012).

Cleary proposes that the AIDA model does not account for the increasingly influential impact of consumer-generated word of mouth, including social media.

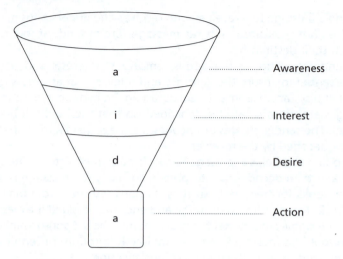

Figure 5.1 The AIDA sales funnel model
Source: St Elmo Lewis, 1898.

While other models describe each stage; in reality the process is not always a straightforward linear sequence. Customers can and do change direction and retrace their steps over the process for more information or reassurance.

Marketers have to choose the right communications tools that are most suitable for the stage which the target audience has reached. For example, traditional advertising may be ideal at raising awareness or creating interest, while complimentary samples and other promotions may be the way to generate a trial. Likewise to build brand qualities, or indeed if you're marketing a financial institution, for example, where free samples are unlikely, sponsorship is a very valuable vehicle for presenting the brand to its customers.

Principles of IMC

There are nine principles of effective integration.

1   Secure board and senior management support for the initiative by ensuring they understand the benefits of IMC and the overarching message.
2   Focus on the customer and direct communications to the buying process. Consider the stages the customer goes through prior to, during and after the purchase. Select the appropriate communications tools for each stage. Plan communications which help the customer move through the stages.
3   Build a budget from scratch, rather than modifying an existing budget. Build a new communications plan. Specify what you need to do in order to achieve your objectives. In reality, the budget you get is often less than you ideally need, so you may have to prioritise communications activities accordingly.
4   Integrate at different levels of the organisation by including 'integration' on the agenda for various internal meetings. This needs to be approached from a

horizontal position to ensure that all managers, not just marketing managers, understand the importance of a consistent message.

5 Focus on a clear marketing communications strategy. Reinforce core values into all communication. Ensure all communications add value to (instead of dilute) the brand or organisation and exploit areas of sustainable competitive advantage.

6 Ensure the design manual or style guide is used to maintain common visual standards for the use of logos, typefaces, colours and so on. Make this widely accessible – limiting access will lead to limited integration.

7 Build relationships and brand values. All communications should help to develop stronger and stronger relationships with customers. Consider how each communication tool helps to build this.

8 Develop a good information system – tools for business. A customer data base, for example, can help the telephone sales area, direct marketing, media agency and sales force. IMC can help to define, collect and share vital information.

9 Share artwork and other media. Consider how, say, advertising imagery can be used in mail shots, signage, business cards, press releases and web sites.

Sponsorship and IMC

There are many great examples of how IMC embraces sponsorship – perhaps this is confirmed by the increase in the number of companies sponsoring events over the past decade. Nevertheless, it is not clear how the effectiveness of event marketing activities can be measured. This is explored in later chapters. Nevertheless, one particular study (Sneath 2005) examined the outcomes associated with an automobile manufacturer's sponsorship of a six-day charitable sporting event. Data for the study came from a sample of 565 spectators in five cities during the six-day event. Results provide evidence for inclusion of event marketing in the company's promotional mix and indicate that experience with the sponsor's products during the event may enhance event outcomes.

Our case study provides similar findings:

Case study 5.1

DHL Rugby World Cup New Zealand 2011

In September 2011, global freight company DHL signed on as a Rugby World Cup 2011 worldwide partner. Their category was 'Official Logistics Partner for Rugby World Cup 2011'. Working with their agencies, DHL created an overarching (integrated marketing communications) campaign strategy to bring to life their role as a partner of the Rugby World Cup 2011.

Although during 2009 DHL was the market leader in the global express and logistics industries, the brand lacked strong brand presence against its competitors (such as FedEx and UPS). As part of their marketing plan for 2010, the brand signed on as a RWC 2011 worldwide partner. They decided to use the sponsorship to build a brand awareness campaign.

This was captured in a simple and powerful platform that allowed for flexible, relevant and compelling communications and engagements across all channels.

To achieve the sponsorship leveraging objectives above, four key areas were focused on:

1 development of a global leverage toolkit for international markets;
2 consumer promotions (these built brand awareness and supported revenue growth);
3 B2B hospitality (this activity built customer loyalty and supported revenue growth); and
4 on ground activation in NZ and Australia.

The strategy – 'Actions speak louder than words', in a nutshell consisted of three core steps to create a compelling brand story and then detonate it.

1 DHL wanted to use its service to play an authentic part in bringing the Rugby World Cup to life, thereby creating a compelling, relevant brand story.
2 Encapsulate this story in a simple platform to be used globally.
3 Bring it to life in multiple channels, including engaging and immersing the audience in the message.

The story was: DHL delivered the necessities that made the tournament a reality. This included 800 tonnes of team equipment to NZ from all 20 competing nations, over 1.4 million tickets worldwide, 130 domestic team freight movements during the tournament and 200 operational movements covering over 30,000 km. And 'All at the Speed of Yellow. DHL – Delivering Rugby to the World'.

While DHL was an official sponsor and the official logistics partner of the Rugby World Cup, they faced numerous challenges in achieving global customer and staff engagement through their leverage and activation at a local and global level.

The challenge

How could DHL:

- Best leverage their sponsorship of the Rugby World Cup 2011 outside New Zealand and achieve significant cut through on a global scale?
- Deliver superior Rugby World Cup 2011 hospitality and create memorable experiences in New Zealand and on Australian shores?

Where should DHL focus their attention with so many markets, matches and locations across so many weeks?

The agency

DHL retained the services of leading Australian activation agency, Traffik Marketing, as lead agency to create and develop an integrated sponsorship activation campaign to ensure that DHL's overall campaign objectives and goals were achieved. HOT Events were responsible for delivering the hospitality programme in New Zealand, and global creative agency 180, with support from advertising agency, Clemenger, Sydney, for the ATL (above the line) benefits.

Overall sponsorship execution elements

At a global level the DHL team in conjunction with their agencies set about delivering the following elements:

- Global toolbox with Rugby World Cup 2011 branded marketing assets for all global markets to utilise.
- Allocating funding to international markets to activate at local level the RWC promotion regarding children of customers and staff with the opportunity to deliver the match ball on-field at key Rugby World Cup 2011 matches.
- Hosting over 3,000 key customers and employees from around the world in NZ, plus a further 17 VIP events in Australia.
- Strategic placement of perimeter boards to ensure maximum DHL visibility on game days.
- Media placement and PR generated by rugby ambassadors – All Black legends Tana Umaga and Sean Fitzpatrick.
- Sponsoring the Rugby World Cup 2011 iPhone app which provides a social media platform.
- Creating a 'DHL RWC 2011 Live Site' in Sydney's Darling Harbour with three large DHL branded screens broadcasting all 48 Foxtel Rugby World Cup games plus local promotion for fans to win tickets to New Zealand by kicking the fastest goal through floating goal posts on the Harbour.
- On the ground in NZ, DHL opted to focus on activities offering maximum fan engagement and brand visibility across all host cities and matches by helping more than 300,000 rugby fans deliver personalised good luck messages to their teams on DHL branded clapper and try banner giveaways.
- Creating activation fan zones to entertain the rugby crowds pre-match with DHL custom built interactive line-out challenges, DHL truck goal kicking simulators and DHL Tana Express digital games on Blackberry Playbooks.
- Conducting online consumer promotions like the Tana Express, giving entrants the chance to play and see how many rugby items ambassador Tana Umaga can load into a moving DHL van. The online game and consumer promotion toured with the NZ Rugby World Cup Trophy Tour where children around the country played for their chance to win the opportunity to deliver the Rugby World Cup 2011 match ball at group stage matches.
- Placing an interactive branded shipping container at the premier fan zone in Queens Wharf, Auckland, for fans to discover DHL's logistical efforts in moving the Rugby World Cup 2011 teams' freight across the globe and within New Zealand. In addition, New Zealand supporters had the opportunity to write a message to the All Blacks on the DHL fan board and perfect their techniques at the DHL kicking simulator.

Communication channels and media

A multi-channel approach was implemented, with each channel targeting a particular segment with a particular objective in mind.

1. Build brand awareness – reach a mass audience

- At a mass audience level, it was all about eyeballs. Via at-stadium elements either directly activated by the agency (e.g. audience supporter visibility items), or designed by the agency (e.g. ground perimeter signage, press conference boards), consumers were also marketed to via television, radio, street banners, NZ newspapers and the 'Tana Express' promotion (explained above) and the 'RWC 2011 Trophy Tour', driven through PR.
- The RWC 'match tracker' on the RWC app was sponsored to target hardcore Rugby fans.
- Additional consumer promotions (explained below) also built brand awareness.
- On ground activations also aided awareness.

2. Customer loyalty – speak directly to the customers

- Customers were marketed to via online communications and RWC 2011 promotional packaging.
- B2B hospitality activity also built customer loyalty.

3. Support revenue growth – existing and prospective clients

The following all supported revenue growth:

- online communications and RWC promotional packaging;
- B2B hospitality;
- consumer promotions;
- on ground activations.

4. Connect with employees – internal engagement

- Staff competitions, promotions to win tickets and internal events engaged staff and delivered a powerful thank you to them.

The sponsorship was regarded as a great success and DHL's research indicates to have lifted it profile through the partnership.

Source: Traffik debrief report

Summary

It seems clear from this chapter that the advent of IMC was instrumental in sponsorship being folded into the marketing operations of sponsor's strategy to build brands, sell products and services and develop relationships with key markets.

Prior to IMC some of these activities took place but not in an integrated and strategic way enabling a more scientific analysis of the sponsorship as an investment against marketing outcomes.

Vignette

Bronze Cola has a very proud history of selling its unique blend of cola drink throughout New Zealand. In the 50 years since they were established they have managed to keep their business on a growth curve and invested in new technology to ensure their production techniques are world class.

While they are a small family company with a turnover of $43 million each year, they decided in 1987 to invest in sponsorship as a way to build their brand profile, to secure exclusive sales opportunities, to engage staff and suppliers and, importantly, to be seen to invest in the communities they rely on.

Sponsorship of the Smiths Beach Classic was the perfect high profile vehicle as the event, the beach and the season were a perfect match. The partnership proved highly entertaining for the sales representatives up and down the country, and was eagerly anticipated by corporate guests, surfers and the general public.

New Zealand hosting the Rugby World Cup in 2011 happened to coincide with the Smiths Beach Classic. Question: The marketing director has decided to entertain his principal clients at the rugby rather than the beach classic; should the managing director intervene and insist on continuing with the tradition? Incidentally, the Rugby World Cup was sponsored by Coca-Cola.

Discussion questions

1 What problems can you see arising out of the IMC approach?
2 Explain the advantages and disadvantages of IMC.
3 What is the difference in the levels of integration, and would some be more acceptable than others?

Bibliography

Angeles Navarro, M. S.-B. (2006) 'Integrated marketing communications: Effects of advertising-sponsorship strategic consistency', *EuroMed Journal of Business*, vol. 4, issue 3, pp. 223–236.

Barry, T. (1986) *Marketing: An Integrated Approach*, The Dydon Press, Chicago.

Belch, G. B. (2004) *Advertising and Promotion: An Integrated Marketing and Communication Perspective*, 3rd edn, McGraw-Hill, Boston.

Cleary, P. (2012) 'Time to update the AIDA model', *B & T*, 1 March, pp. 4–5.

Faulds, W. M. (2009) 'Social media: The new hybrid element of the promotions mix', *Business Horizons*, vol. 52, issue 4, July–August, pp. 357–365.

Grohs, R., Wagner, U. and Vsetecka, S. (2004) 'Assessing the effectiveness of sports sponsorships: An empirical examination', *Schamalenbach Business Review*, vol. 56, April 2004, pp. 119–138.

Holm, O. (2006) 'Competitive strategy, marketing communications, marketing strategy, Sweden', *Corporate Communications: An International Journal*, vol. 11, issue 1, pp. 23–33.

James, B. (1972) *Integrated Marketing*, Penguin, Harmondsworth.

Kelly, L. and Whiteman, C. (2010) 'Sports sponsorship as an IMC tool: An Australian sponsor's perspective', *Journal of Sponsorship*, vol. 4, no. 1, pp. 26–33.

Kitchen, P. (1997) 'Integrated marketing communications in U.S. advertising agencies: An exploratory study', *Journal of Advertising Research*, September–October, pp. 7–18.

——(2005) 'New paradigm – IMC – under fire', *Competitiveness Review: An International Business Journal of Global Competitiveness*, vol. 15, issue 1, pp. 72–80.

Moor, E. T. (1992) *Integrated Communication: Synergy of Persuasive Voices*, Lawrence Erlbaum Associates, Mahwah, NJ.

Morley, I. A. (1995) *Integrated Marketing Communications*, Butterworth Heinemann, Oxford.

Phelps, J. N. (2005) 'Conceptualising the integrated marketing communications phenomenon: An examination of its impact on advertsing practises', in Kitchen, P. J., De Pelsmacher, P., Schultz, D. E. and Eagle, L. K., eds, *A Reader in Marketing Communications*, Routledge, New York.

Prakash Vel, R. S. (2010) 'Megamarketing an event using integrated marketing communications: The success story of TMH', *Business Strategy Series*, vol. 11, issue 6, pp. 371–382.

Shaw, R. S. (1981) *Marketing: An Integrated Analytical Approach*, South Western Publishing, Cincinnati, OH.

Sneath, R. Z. (2005) 'An IMC approach to event marketing: The effects of sponsorship and experiance on customer attitudes', *Journal of Advertising Research*, vol. 45, pp. 373–381.

Speed, R. and Thompson, P. (2000) 'Determinants of sports sponsorship response', *Journal of the Academy of Marketing Science*, vol. 28, no. 2, pp. 227–238.

Sreedhar Madhavaram, V. B. (2005) 'Integrated marketing communication (IMC) and brand identity as critical components of brand equity strategy: A conceptual framework and research propositions', *Journal of Advertising*, vol. 34, no. 4, pp. 69–80.

St Elmo Lewis, E. (1898) 'The AIDA sales funnel model', available at: www.proven-models.com/547/aida-sales-funnel/

Taylor, C. (2010) 'Intergated marketing communications in 2010 and beyond', *International Journal of Advertising*, vol. 29, issue 2, pp. 161–164.

Walliser, B. (2003) 'An international review of sponsorship research: Extension and update', *International Journal of Advertising*, vol. 22, no. 1, pp. 5–40.

Chapter 6

The sponsorship proposal

Learning outcomes

After reading and discussing the contents of this chapter, students will be able to:

- identify the differences between a sponsorship proposal and prospectus;
- identify five elements that should be included in the sponsorship proposal;
- show how IMC connects to the sponsorship proposal.

Introduction

Sponsorship proposals take many forms; they can be elaborate and highly polished documents or they can be modest project outlines. Nevertheless, however they are constructed, they are a direct reflection of the property they are representing. They are, like all material generated, a statement about the property and therefore need careful consideration.

As we have learnt earlier, sponsorship is an important marketing and communication tool commonly used by organisations. Companies sponsor events with the intention of making a measurable financial return. When soliciting sponsorship it is essential to persuade prospective sponsors how the business's goals interact with the proposal. To that end, the sponsorship proposal is actually a business proposal that must help the sponsor accomplish their business goals.

Two approaches

Sponsorship proposals tend to be in two forms – targeted and highly researched documents, or broadly distributed ones – or, to use common parlance, as the sniper or the shotgun approach. Depending on time, the property and the financial and other expectations, one method might be preferable to the other.

For clarity it is best to refer to the untargeted, generic package as the *sponsorship prospectus* and the targeted package as the *sponsorship proposal*. Both of these packages are referred to as 'decks'.

The development of an asset list is a valuable start in the development of either of these documents. This involves identifying the assets and opportunities that may be included in the offering. Broadly, assets might involve areas such as:

- marketing exposure – such as logo or product advertising – both at the event and in the pre- and post-campaign;
- hospitality – client entertainment, staff entertainment at the event;
- promotional opportunities – both before, during and after the event.

Most of the generic property information will be the same and in some cases the negotiations will commence with the property outline, including target audience, marketing plan and other relevant information.

Sponsorship prospectus

The 'prospectus' should be used as a credentials document, something that pulls together all relevant facts about the activity, background on the organisation and key figures and other facts to add credibility that the property will be well run.

This sort of document is not dissimilar to sales tools used in other industries, for example, those for a car. When visiting a showroom of new motor vehicles the event producers are offered a brochure of the vehicle with the specifications, a couple of wonderful photos and other design devices to make the product alluring. A similar form is used for selling a sponsorship property.

The ideal scenario is to present this at a meeting and to get feedback about whether initially the event fits within the company's plans, whether the market or audience are the right fit and whether there are other clashing or complementary activities planned during the same period.

Another key piece of information to extract from the meeting is who is the ultimate decision maker. There may be more than one as it can be one person's role to approve the budget, i.e. the marketing director, and another's to run the relationship and approve elements after the initial resource commitment, such as a brand manager. Increasingly agencies are being briefed by clients to represent them in sponsorship.

How far the event producer can second guess, and how responsible the event producer should be for generating ideas for leveraging the property, will differ from prospect to prospect; nevertheless, there is little doubt that from both sides of the agreement the more integrated the leveraging the better outcome for both parties.

All of the feedback provides great insight into the development of the sponsorship proposal.

Sponsorship proposal

The sponsorship proposal is a document that has been prepared with one prospect in mind. It is a document that is very particular about the partnership. It will have involved significant research from various sources on the prospect's strategy, brand and past budgets. It will have involved meetings with various people involved in the process, such as the marketing or sponsorship manager, advertising agencies, activations agencies, etc., to ensure that the proposal meets the appropriate objectives.

Given the time spent on the development of the proposal, it is important that the prospect is aware that the proposal is being prepared. The proposal should outline:

Target markets

Who are the audiences of the event? What are the target markets? Where do they come from and how does the event producer reach them? How do they relate to the prospective sponsor's markets?

Delivery of benefits

Sometimes the easy part of sponsorship is the sales part, the hunting and capture from either the sponsor or the event owner, although it can involve some stressful moments of negotiation. Once the sponsorship is confirmed, the promises have to be delivered and often there are elements within the deal that were not fully foreseen – by either side.

Sponsorship package

The sponsorship package is the name given to the detailing in the proposal – what each party provides the other in terms of exchange. So generally the event owner provides brand association and or product marketing exposure, whether from a business to consumer (B2C) or business to business (B2B) market, and hospitality for entertaining – which may be for internal relations, or to reward key stakeholders.

Preparation

Sponsorships are hard work and should not be seen as an easy way to raise funds for projects or to keep the event producer in a solid financial position. Sponsorship is a business arrangement, which yields a commercial return for the sponsor. In order to succeed it is essential that the event owner is able to prove to a prospective sponsor that it is a worthy partner that is going to deliver tangible benefits and results. Once the sponsorship is secured, the hard work really starts. Before the sales process and the development of the proposal there are a number of internal considerations:

- Ensure the organisation is prepared for the association with a corporate sponsor. Everyone in the organisation – including board members, performers, players, administrators, volunteers – has a role to play as an ambassador at the least or as neutral at worst.
- Once a corporate expresses interest in negotiating, who has the authority to negotiate and to what extent?

There are always some corporates that provide an uncomfortable alignment for the event owner, such as children's sport and fast food. A focused sponsorship sales representative may not be wise enough to consider the wider implications of a sponsorship; they may only be concerned with reaching the income target at any cost. It is therefore worthwhile investing the time in the development of a sponsorship policy. This policy should include:

- organisation's objectives;
- administrative processes involved with a sponsorship, e.g. approvals, contracts, review, promotional activities and evaluation;
- naming rights and issues around duration of a naming rights deal;
- accountability and responsibility;
- exclusivity in category;
- specific issues relevant to the property such as exclusions, e.g. tobacco and alcohol industry and limitations.

Staff resources

Resourcing is also a key element to consider in the cost of sponsorship, because sponsors will have expectations that the relationship will be managed on a professional level and that they will have a centralised point of contact.

Marketing plan

Early on in the negotiations, if a marketing plan is not already a key component of the sponsorship proposal it will be necessary to present one. If this is not finalised by the time the proposal is being prepared a draft plan will be sufficient, particularly if it is backed up with a date when the final plan will be available. From a sponsor perspective this demonstrates:

- the event is well run;
- there is some guaranteed exposure;
- the market of the media will align with the audience at the event.

Audience profile

An essential element of the sponsorship proposal is a profile on the audience for the event. If the event is new it is essential that the event producer explain who the audience will be and how this might be justified.

The audience profile ideally will be both demographic and psychographic, and if the event is not new, it would be valuable to reveal information from post-event research such as feedback from the previous event.

Organisation audit

It may also be useful to include in the proposal a SWOT (strengths, weaknesses, opportunities, threats) analysis of the event producer. This would outline in brief what the event producer's competitors are doing and who their sponsors are. This provides the prospective sponsor with an idea of the professionalism of the organisation and how they might use the sponsorship, and how the event will develop its selling position.

Developing the benefits package

In general terms, a sponsor wants three things from an event owner:

1 *Image association*: to be associated with the event's core values and attributes with the goal being to introduce or reinforce those attributes within its company or product.
2 *Target audience*: to access one or more of the event's target markets and to reach these people with the sponsor's marketing message in a meaningful way.
3 *Tangible benefits*: to gain a range of benefits from the event, ensuring the impact of the previous two elements is maximised and providing mechanisms and tools to achieve specific marketing objectives.

In order to maximise the event's chances of creating a strong match with a sponsor, it is imperative that there is a deep understanding of what can be offered in each of these areas, and the more precisely these benefits can be described, the better.

An effective proposal does require creativity and the capacity to find the unique 'money-can't-buy' opportunity and exploit the link between the event and the sponsor.

Sponsorship 'hierarchy'

Another aspect of preparation for sponsorship is deciding what the financial requirement is and the structure of the sponsorship hierarchy. This may involve both a financial and an in-kind perspective.

For example, the event producer may choose to find sponsors for particular projects or spaces. One model is *naming rights* (e.g. Qantas Lounge at the Museum of Contemporary Art in Sydney, Citi Performing Arts Centre in Boston, Man Booker Prize) or association with a production or exhibition or season (season proudly brought to the event producer by sponsor).

Another model is the *tiered approach* (e.g. lead sponsor, major sponsor, and supporting sponsor) for the event producer; or a decision to have one sole sponsor.

Another alternative is to follow the Olympic example and offer a *level playing field*, exclusive in clearly defined categories.

It is essential that all benefits are clearly defined for each level so that there is no confusion as to entitlement and sponsorship levels.

Establishing value

The third step in the 'packaging' stage, and probably the most difficult, is confirming what the sponsorship is worth. This can be looked at in three ways:

- *The real cost to the event producer* (benefits provided, staff and administration, sale costs). After the real costs are identified these should then be added to the margin or profit the organisation hopes to achieve. As a guideline, this may be 100 per cent added to total cost of sponsorship.
- *The market price.* Ensure the sponsorship is correctly valued in the marketplace. Check on what similar organisations/properties are charging. Review the sponsorship opportunity to ensure the comparison in like for like (benefits, audience reach, profile, marketing support).
- *Compare with mainstream media costs.* How much would it cost a sponsor to reach the same audience through, for example, direct mail, television, online, outdoor and print media advertisements, etc.?

The dilemma of contra

Contra or in-kind sponsorship (where a company's products or services are provided in lieu of, or as well as, cash) can be a most useful alternative for some event producers. Nevertheless the sponsorship needs to assist the event producer's bottom line, e.g. budgeted expenditure not unbudgeted expenditure.

How the contra is valued becomes another policy issue, whether it is costed at retail price or at the company's budgeted cost or wholesale price. Depending on where the event is staged there may also be important tax issues to consider with in-kind sponsorships.

Carrying it off

Step 1 – creating a hit list

The first step in finding potential sponsors is creating a hit list. This can be approached in three ways:

- *Audience*: know the audience first and then identify companies that want to reach that audience in a meaningful way.
- *Objectives*: which companies are trying to achieve the same goals as the event, e.g. an innovative event could tie in with an IT company.
- *Attributes*: which companies would like to think that they share attributes with the event, e.g. glamorous cosmetics company may like the image of a contemporary dance company.

When an organisation is identified that fits all three areas, then there is the potential for a good sponsorship fit.

To develop this list further is all about research. Sometimes knowing the personalities in senior roles at the prospective sponsors is useful in gathering likely supporters of the proposal. However, the most important person is the one with the budget sign-off responsibility.

The prospect list should be explored further, and this would involve seeking sponsorship guidelines for the prospective sponsors to check whether the property fits the requirements. For example, if the event is a sportsperson, the event producer will find that some companies mention in their policy that they will not support individuals; if the event is held on a Sunday, there are companies that cannot be involved with the event; and if the event is a family event the event producer is unlikely to secure alcohol sponsorship.

The identification of prospective sponsors tends towards those sponsors that are consumer facing (B2C), because they are the big marketers. This can sometimes lead to overlooking the substantial B2B markets, and often these are harder to identify. Sometimes in this situation an event producer can utilise their board to approach suggested organisations, because they can sometimes provide the all-important foot in the door.

Step 2 – developing the proposal

Once the hit list is constructed, the proposal needs to be prepared. Unlike the prospectus, the proposal needs to be personalised.

The information the event producer requires from a company, such as its communication objectives, target audiences and sponsorship criteria, can be difficult to obtain. Possible recourses, however, are to review their web site; read their annual report; ask the receptionist for a mission statement; find out who else they sponsor; and research the prospective sponsor's advertising campaigns. All this information should assist in tailoring a sponsorship proposal that will be on track from a marketing perspective.

Try not to make it too long (no more than ten pages with benefits). Ideally provide a summary at the beginning of the proposal with a strong graphic – a photo or design that is attention drawing.

This means that the reader may recall the proposal when following up and will assist in their own selection of proposals.

Step 3 – selling the sponsorship

The sponsorship sales process can be quite lengthy and requires much patience and perseverance.

Depending on the sponsor's business cycle and plans, the process may take from three months to a year. It would be a mistake to pursue only one prospect at a time, being preferable to explore multiple prospects, it may be that the event producer can accommodate only one but take it off the market once the sponsor has confirmed in writing.

Sponsorship sales, like all proactive selling, require perseverance and sensitivity in avoiding annoyance, and must always be succinct as to why this sponsorship stands apart from the other proposals from other organisations they may be considering.

When a meeting is scheduled, ensure that the appropriate level of personnel are in attendance; for example, if presenting to their CEO, ensure that the general manager/director or board member is present.

Step 4 – servicing the sponsorship

Once a sponsor has 'signed up', the exacting part begins. It is essential that the agreement or contract is prepared to involve other parts of the event producer's business such as financial, legal and marketing. Their role is directly or indirectly referred to in the agreement, as well as those who are indirectly responsible for the deliverables outlined in the agreement. Additionally the agreement or contract needs to cover sponsorship cost, duration, benefits and termination clauses.

Ideally a sponsorship servicing plan will be developed. This will assist both parties throughout the sponsorship term and ensure a successful relationship is established.

The most successful sponsorships are those that are integrated into the sponsor's overall communication plans and vehicles. It will be up to the person dedicated to servicing sponsorships to always be on the watch for opportunities where the sponsor can maximise its investment as the relationship progresses, whether it be through the event producer's own marketing/PR communications or through cross-promoting with other sponsors.

Sponsorships work best when nurtured and developed over a period of time. By working closely with sponsors, setting clear objectives and performance benchmarks and delivering the agreed benefits and desired outcomes, the partnership has a future.

Looking at the event marketing plan from a sponsor's perspective

For an event producer, always write and read proposals and other material from the perspective of someone who knows little about the organisation or event. Do not assume knowledge, or passion.

- *Target audiences*: What shared or new audiences will a sponsor reach through the property?
- *Market research*: What is the event's relationship with its audience and how will this benefit a sponsor? For example, is there a membership, fan club, supporter group, volunteers?
- *Internal analysis*: Is the event producer ready to work with a sponsor? Are all departments/key personnel on-side and staff clearly briefed as to what is required?
- *Environmental analysis*: Why should a sponsor choose an arts organisation over, say, a sporting body?

- *Competitor analysis*: Why would a company sponsor one event over a competitor's? For example, can sponsoring one event block a sponsor's competitor from reaching the same market?
- *Marketing SWOT analysis*: What strengths and opportunities can the event producer bring to a sponsor's own marketing strategies and communications?
- *Marketing strategies*: What are the existing channels for a sponsor to communicate with the event producer's audience?
- *Evaluation*: How will a sponsor know if the sponsorship is successful? Possible signs are improved brand awareness; financial return on investment; key business contacts formed, etc.

Benefits inventory

- *Exclusivity*: Can the event producer offer sponsor category exclusivity within its industry group (e.g. one financial institution, one airline, one car company)?
- *Naming rights to the event*: If this can be offered, what is the minimum term or duration and what notice is required from the sponsor to end the relationship?
- *What are the event producer's core brand values*? If the event producer was a person, how would the event audience describe it (e.g. clever, sexy, sophisticated, fun, family-orientated, healthy)?
- *Target audience*: Clearly define the event target audience/s, by both demographics and psychographics. Who will hear the sponsor's message?
- *Signage*: What is possible, what is the producer providing and what additional opportunities are there for sponsors (e.g. banners on outside of building; within venue; free-standing signs; plaques; an artwork incorporating sponsor logo/company name)? Be creative and be specific about size and placement.
- *Media/marketing exposure*: What is the event producer doing to promote the sponsor's product? How will the event producer acknowledge the sponsor within the communication vehicles? Possibilities include advertising, marketing and promotional material, and direct mail.
- *PR opportunities*: What is the PR strategy? How will sponsors be acknowledged to the media and general public?
- *Marketing and promotional tie-ins*: What programmes of the event producers can the sponsor tie into? What cross-promotions could they undertake with co-sponsors or other suppliers of the event producers?
- *Corporate hospitality*: What opportunities can the event producer offer for client entertaining?
- *Networking*: Can the event producer offer invitations to prestigious or interesting events?
- *Employee involvement*: How can the event producer involve the sponsor's employees (e.g. free tickets, employee family days, workshops for employees' children)?
- *Function facilities*: Can the event producer offer free venue hire?
- *Ticketing*: How many complimentary tickets/passes or invitations can the event producer offer to a sponsor?
- *Merchandising rights*: Can a sponsor co-brand any merchandise the event producer may produce for the project?
- *Sampling*: Is there the opportunity for the sponsor to sample product at the venue, or direct mail to the event producer's data base?

- *Endorsement*: Are there any personalities/'stars' from the event producer who could endorse a sponsor's product or participate in their advertising/marketing programmes?
- *Integration*: Are there any other activities that can be brought together (e.g. a performance on-site, using sponsor's products or the sponsor offering trainee roles for returned performers/players)?

Sponsorship proposal template

Executive summary

Tell them in a paragraph or two the unique reason why they should support the event producer's proposal. In a nutshell, what's in it for them?

Background on company

Keep it to one page and make it short, sharp and interesting. Include the event producer's mission statement.

Background on event

Again, keep it to one page. What is this project all about from their point of view? What will a partnership achieve for them?

Market research

Include as much relevant market research as possible on the organisation or project, at the very least a detailed audience profile: who they are, their income and education levels, where they live, etc. Who will the sponsor reach and how is this unique opportunity to reach them?

The pitch

Invite the participation of the prospect company. Spell out exactly what the event producer wants from them and exactly what the event producer will provide. This should include price of sponsorship (cash and/or in-kind), what level of sponsorship they will receive, where they will sit within the sponsorship hierarchy, what period it covers and payment due dates.

The benefits

Outline in as much detail as possible what is on offer in return for the price. These benefits may need to be further tailored and included in a follow-up document.

Marketing plan

Outline what the event producer is doing to promote the project advertising, publicity, editorial, contra media sponsorship.

Organisation inventory

Audience

- How many visitors per year/exhibition/show, etc.?
- Audience demographics – from where, age group, profile.
- What research is/has been undertaken on visitors?

Membership

- Does the event producer organisation have a membership programme?
- How many, what levels, what involvement?
- How often does the event producer communicate with them? Does the event producer know if they appreciated it; are there feedback mechanisms in place?
- What communications channels does the event producer have, e.g. emails, newsletters, functions, mailouts?

Mailing list

- size, who is on it, how is it used?
- what are the data base capabilities – what program, etc.?

Current/past sponsors

- who, what level, ongoing commitment?
- cash or in-kind?
- are there links from board members?

Government support

- to what extent – cash or in kind? Core funding or project funding?
- how stable is the political climate?
- key supporters?

Board/patrons

- are there any prominent members?
- are there any key government players at particular events?

Sister/linked organisations

- what is the link?
- how can we work with what they are doing?
- what is their membership/audience profile?

Image

- what is USP (unique selling point) and brand values?
- how does the audience see the event producer?
- how does the membership base see the event producer?
- how does the board see the event producer?

Sponsorship targets

- what is the event producer sponsorship $$ targets?
- what are the event producer in-kind needs – the ones that add real value and those that save $$?
- what levels are available – e.g. naming rights, tiers, membership?

Benefits

- exposure (what advertising/marketing/PR planned?);
- hospitality (openings, private viewings, cocktails, mix with other sponsors, government representation);
- staff involvement (discounts, free passes, employee days, voluntary positions, functions and events, lectures, artists as speakers, conferences, workshops).

Partnerships/cross promotions

- what other events or activities are happening at the same time and location as the sponsorship, e.g. arts festivals, football season, fairs, exhibitions and shows, that the event producer could cross-promote with?
- who is the competition?
- what are they doing?

Marketing and advertising

- schedules, what planned, to what dollar value, reach;
- television, radio, print, press, Internet site, newsletter, outdoor – posters, banners, on-site/off-site, education material;
- flyers, invitations, catalogues, room displays, room brochures;
- PR strategy.

On-site

- where would sponsor be acknowledged, e.g. inside/outside venue space?
- What can sponsor provide to aid exposure, e.g. banners, displays, product, prizes, inserts in mailings?

Useful printed information for preparing the proposal

- background about the event producer organisation;
- past annual reports;
- past marketing materials, e.g. invitations, newsletters, posters, catalogues, ads;

- past media clippings on institution plus awards;
- past sponsorship reports (if undertaken).

Sponsorship servicing plan

Clearly outline the objectives of the sponsoring organisation. This will assist both the event producer and the sponsor in evaluating the sponsorship results, and gives the event producer a referral point throughout the sponsorship.

- Set lines of communication: Who from the event producer's organisation will be involved in servicing the sponsorship, and who is their correlating staff contact point at the sponsoring organisation?
- Set reporting mechanisms: How and when is the event producer going to report on the sponsorship? Who from the event producer will be involved? For example, three-monthly written reports prepared by the sponsorship manager, including media clippings prepared by the PR manager.
- Set benchmarks, agreed by both the event producer and the sponsor, that indicate what will make the partnership successful, e.g. 1,000 people through the door each month; or 40 per cent audience sponsor recall at end of project; or 10 per cent increase in sales leads through the event producer venue.
- Set evaluation mechanisms: How is the event producer going to evaluate whether the benchmarks have been met and whether the sponsorship is successful (e.g. visitor exit surveys/seat drops; direct mail follow-up; focus groups; tagged direct mail/coupons)?
- Clearly outline the benefits package for each sponsor within the plan, and then ensure that all are delivered.
- Ensure artwork and marketing materials are approved by the sponsor within adequate (pre-agreed) lead times.
- Ensure sponsors are on media distribution list and VIP invitation list. Ensure they are invited to *all* key functions during the sponsorship term, even if they do not relate directly to their project.
- Hold regular meetings and involve other key staff where relevant, e.g. curatorial/creative staff to give updates on the exhibition or show. This makes the sponsor feel more involved with the project and makes for more interesting meetings.
- Put everything in writing. Take contact reports at meetings.
- Conduct research: As per evaluation methods confirmed.
- Keep media clippings and/or electronic media references (where relevant – especially if sponsor is mentioned); copies of advertisements; testimonials; visitors' comments.

Summary

There are a number of steps in developing a sponsorship proposal:

1 Obtain sponsorship guidelines of the prospective sponsor and other intelligence about the marketing activities or initiatives to give the event producer a glimpse into the review and evaluation criteria of the prospective sponsors. The guidelines

may also provide information regarding submission deadlines, eligibility, proposal review time frame and contact information. It is likely that there will be many other organisations seeking sponsorship, so if the event producer decided to proceed with the proposal in a non-preferred manner the sponsor may be more likely to dismiss the proposal. Make sure the proposal names people correctly.

2 Remember that one of the sponsor's motives is to raise their profile. The research undertaken must help build an understanding of the mission of the event producer and prospective sponsor. The background information in the guides will assist in the construction of a proposal that will be easy to skim for key points such as the nature of the event, how much it costs and what the sponsor stands to gain. Avoid writing a high-priced or an over-packaged proposal.

3 Include an abstract or summary in the main proposal which must offer a concise description of the project, objectives and the possible outcome. Use available statistics and data from newspapers and news magazines in the main part to support the proposal.

4 The aim is for the event producer proposal to be read thoroughly by prospects the event producer approaches. Keep the rhetoric about the event producer organisation to a minimum. Avoid making implicit promises. If the event producer thinks the event will boost the event producer sponsor's sales or corporate image, the event producer must knowledgeably show that in the event producer proposal.

Bibliography

Cornwall, T. B. (2008) 'State of art and science in sponsorship-linked marketing', *Journal of Advertising*, vol. 37, no. 3, pp. 41–55.

Dolphin, R. R. (2003) *Sponsorship: Perspectives on its Strategic Role*, MUP UP Ltd, Northampton.

Drennan, J. C. and Cornwell, T. B. (2004) 'Emerging strategies for sponsorship on the internet', *Journal of Marketing Management*, vol. 20, nos. 9–10, pp. 1123–1146.

Geldard, E. and Sinclair, L. (2002) *The Sponsorship Manual: Sponsorship Made Easy*, The Sponsorship Unit, Upper Ferntree Gully, VIC, Australia.

Manda. G. (2012) 'How to write an event sponsorship proposal'. Retrieved 25 October 2012, from www.ehow.com/how 7781272 write-event-sponsorship-proposal. html#ixzz1hmtpYRhX

Oberauer, K. (2012) 'Practical sponsorship ideas'. Retrieved 5 October, 2012, from www.htp//practicalsponsorshipideas.com.blog

Parker, K. (1991) 'Sponsorship: The research contribution', *European Journal of Marketing*, vol. 25, no. 11, pp. 22–30.

Rifon, N. J., Choi, S. M., Trimble, C. S. and Li, H. (2004) 'Congruence effects in sponsorship: The mediating role of sponsor credibility and consumer attributions of sponsor motive', *Journal of Advertising*, vol. 33, no. 1, pp. 30–42.

Sunshine, K. M. (1995) 'An examination of sponsorship proposals in relation to corporate objectives', *Festival Management and Event Tourism*, vol. 2, numbers 3–4, pp. 159–166.

Chapter 7

Managing the sponsorship

Learning outcomes

After reading and discussing the contents of this chapter, students will be able to:

- define the purpose of the sponsorship contract;
- describe what ambush marketing is and measures to minimise exposure to ambush;
- outline the importance of the sponsorship management plan.

Introduction

A contract can sound very onerous and serious; nevertheless, a contract is an essential part of forming a business relationship. It is simply an agreement entered into without coercion by two or more parties who intend to create legal obligations between or among them. The *elements* of a contract are 'offer' and 'acceptance' by 'competent persons' having legal capacity who exchange 'consideration' to create 'mutuality of obligation'. These principles extend to other forms of agreement.

Sponsorship agreements

Sometimes an instrument such as a memorandum of understanding (MOU) or letter of agreement is used to outline in writing the terms of the deal. Skildum-Reid (Skildum-Reid and Grey 2008) identifies four types of agreement:

- drawn up by a lawyer and signed by both parties with company seal;
- proforma signed by both parties with company seal;
- letter of agreement signed by both parties;
- confirmation letter.

Most often the more significant the value or term of the agreement, the more detailed the agreement needs to be. For example, many organisations have thresholds for the letter of agreement requiring a contract beyond $50,000 expenditure.

Contracts surround us every day, from the tiny words on the back of train tickets to the enormity of a home mortgage, or even a mobile phone contract. They are therefore very standard and not something to be alarmed by; nevertheless, from time to time the language used can seem more complicated than necessary.

A contract is simply an agreement entered into voluntarily by two parties or more with the intention of creating a legal obligation. It is possible for a contract to be made orally but in this context we will focus on a written contract.

The contract outlines the responsibilities of the parties, the terms of the relationship, and the terms for renewal. It will also deal with the failure by one party to deliver their contracted responsibilities; this is referred to as a breach of contract.

Breach of contract

A breach (or breaking) of contract can be lead to 'damages' or compensation of money or other agreed value. This will be spelt out in the contract, as may be the termination of the contract. It will depend on the parties if not defined in the contract. In equity law, the remedy can be specific performance of the contract or an injunction. Both of these remedies award the party at loss the 'benefit of the bargain' or expectation damages, which are greater than mere reliance damages, as in promissory estoppels.

A breach of contract is the main dispute trigger between the contracted parties; nevertheless, there are other situations where disputes may be significant enough for formal consideration. These need to be considered and included in the contract.

There are four stages to resolving a breach of contract: the most obvious response is conversation, which need only involve the sponsor and the property owner – it should be noted that the steps that follow all involve payment for services to assist in finding a solution, depending on the value or loss of value caused by the breach or indeed capacity to pay.

If the conversation does not resolve the breach, the issue can escalate to mediation, where an outsider (mediator) considers the issues of the two parties and proposes a resolution, but neither party is bound to the mediator's ruling; arbitration, again involving an outsider (arbitrator) but where both parties agree in advance to abide by the ruling of the arbitrator; and finally to litigation – there is no quick fix in this process, which involves substantial time and financial commitment.

Contract

A contract is a legally enforceable promise or undertaking that something will or will not occur. The word 'promise' can be used as a legal synonym for contract; although care is required as a promise may not have the full standing of a contract, e.g. when it is an agreement without consideration.

Contract law varies greatly from one jurisdiction to another, including differences in common law compared to civil law, the impact of received law, particularly from England in common law countries, and of law codified in regional legislation.

Regarding Australian contract law, for example, there are 40 relevant Acts which impact on the interpretation of contract at the Commonwealth (federal/national) level, and an additional 26 acts at the level of the State of New South Wales. In addition there are six international instruments or conventions which are applicable for international dealings, such as the United Nations Convention on Contracts for the International Sale of Goods (Vienna Sales Convention).

Event producers are surrounded by contracts. In fact all business relies on contracts. Event producer's contracts will need to be in place for many different resources in order to realise the events – venues, artists, players, judges, staff, advertising, consultants – all these involve contracts or agreements.

In fact many of the benefits or opportunities offered in sponsorship arrangements rely on other parties delivering the benefit; for example, player or artist participation in functions and content arrangements where distribution rights are provided. The ability to offer these opportunities needs to be outlined and clarified in the contract.

Generally the party seeking the sponsorship will issue the contract after significant discussion and negotiation. If the relationship is ongoing, covering multiple seasons, the specific details of the partnership might be covered in a schedule, a document attached to the contract.

When dealing with major corporate sponsors there is a good chance they will take on the details of the event producer's contract and input them into their own form of contract.

Preparing a contract is good discipline, it ensures that many questions are investigated and the downstream elements are brought to light before the contract is executed. From both party's perspectives, preparation of a detailed contract ensures the rules are in place before the event. In most cases the contract literally becomes a bottom drawer document, meaning it is not referred to but is just there for safekeeping.

Contents of a contract

- clear understanding of the expectations of each partner;
- primary objectives for both partners;
- the benefits to be exchanged – what, when, how and how much;
- requirements for communications and reporting – what, by whom and when;
- how the relationship will be managed and by whom;
- the process for evaluation, how it will be done and by whom;
- process for approvals for marketing and promotional materials, guest lists, etc.;
- process for review;
- process for dealing with disputes;
- process for terminating the agreement.

The sponsorship contract needs to incorporate the following considerations

- *Exclusivity in category*: It cannot be assumed what the other party thinks in this regard. For example, a soft drink manufacturer may see their category as being across all drink unless it is specifically defined as non-alcoholic carbonated beverages. Banks could, unless defined and agreed separately, call on the financial services category including insurance and non-bank credit providers.
- *Exclusivity in territory*: Part of the negotiation involves whether the sponsorship is for national, international or other territory. This is likely to have some impact on the sponsorship fee and essentially can mean there may be different partners for different territories. This will have some impact, mainly on the use of intellectual property (IP).

Term of contract

There are a number of time-related issues to consider in the contract:

Payment

The property owner will always want to receive as much of the sponsorship fee as possible in advance of the event. In many cases this is much to do with ensuring sufficient cash flow to fund the activity. The sponsor on the other hand prefers to pay slowly as it keeps some control, and should the sponsorship fail to deliver the outcomes anticipated the sponsor gains a position of advantage in the conversations that follow.

The usual scenario is to split the payments, part on signing, part on commencement of the event and part on receipt of the event report. These are not necessarily equal instalments.

Details such as the process for the fund transfer need to be discussed well before the due dates, as each sponsor will have their own peculiarities in terms of accounts receivable and payment terms.

Renewal

It is usual that the 'first' rights of renewal are reserved for the sponsor and the dates by which the renewal needs to be confirmed are outlined in the contract. It is also often the case that 'last' rights be included as well.

First rights are pretty clear – the event producer is required to offer the sponsorship opportunity to the current sponsor before offering it to another party. Only when the current sponsor declines – and timing for this should be stipulated in the agreement – can other parties be approached. Needless to say, there will be some changes to the property and in the sponsorship fee.

Last rights are not as clear – having declined to renew the sponsorship on the terms proposed, the current sponsor can insist on being given an offer at the end of the sales process as well. The main objective is that the sponsorship fee is likely to have been reduced over the sales period; this would be to the sponsor's advantage.

Annual review of sponsorship investment

Multi-year agreements need to incorporate an annual increment in sponsorship fees. These are often tied back to national indices such as the consumer price index (CPI) in Australia. This measures annual percentage changes in the cost of living for consumers and when applied to the base level sponsorship ensures the value of the sponsorship – or the buying power remains of equal value.

It might be that in securing the sponsorship, the first year was made available at a low entry price, with a significant increase in year two; nevertheless, the annual increment is based on the buying power of the dollar, not on the value of the property.

Contingency arrangements

This clause is to cover for things that cannot be foreseen; for example, a change in legislation or a change in business performance. In recent years actions by individual members of sporting teams have led to sponsors withdrawing their sponsorship through this sort of clause where changed circumstances have allowed early exit.

Checklists

The following checklist (Geldard and Sinclair 2002) for contract content is not comprehensive but should be seen as a guide to ensure major elements have not been overlooked in the preparation of the contract. It should not be used in place of professional legal advice.

Parties
(a) Full names of the parties included in the contract; these need to be the legal business names as well as appropriate business trading numbers.
(b) Names of the chief executives and the principal point of contact for each party need to be included in the contract.

Property
(a) Describe the nature of the event, whether the sponsorship is of an organisation, event, team, individual or venue.
(b) Describe the regulations, if any, that the contract is using to interpret the event, more applicable to sporting than cultural events.
(c) Describe the nature of the event.
(d) Details required of attendance of particular personalities or artists.

(e) Geographic boundaries of the event.
(f) Dates and times of the event.
(g) Venue for the event.

Term
(a) Length of time of the agreement.
(b) Date of commencement.
(c) Right of renewal, and dates for confirmation and terms and conditions of renewal.

Sponsorship rights and benefits
(a) Level of exclusivity.
(b) Relationship to other sponsors – if any.
(c) Naming rights or presenting rights sponsors have the right to their name being included in the name of the event.
(d) Major sponsors rights to exclusivity. Exclusivity in use of IP or in sales of product.

Publicity

Elements of publicity and media management should be clarified in the sponsorship management plan. Nevertheless, it is usually the case that the publicity function for the property focuses on developing media coverage of the event, doing everything in their power to incorporate sponsor branding or references in the stories.

They are likely to appeal to specialist writers or writers of general early news, depending on the event. Sponsor's publicists might be more likely to use their relationships and look for coverage in financial pages or industry media outside of the interest or contact base of the event publicists.

While it is in everyone's interest to generate as much media coverage as possible, it is also essential to capture all the media by media monitoring.

Corporate entertainment

Not long ago corporate entertainment was the major driver in sponsorships; while it is still of great significance it has lost the position of being the most significant element. Nevertheless, in sectors like professional services (accountants, lawyers, etc.) which are not consumer facing and are sometimes referred to as business to business (B2B), high level entertainment and 'money can't buy' experiences are key to sponsorship success.

Skildum-Reid (Skildum-Reid and Grey 2008) noted that there is a plethora of invitations to events to key business people and due to their similarity – sitting in a corporate box, at a special dinner, an opening night of theatre or around the 18 holes at a golf tournament – the outcome of being a memorable and shared experience can be lost amongst all the other activities.

So the 'money can't buy' experience is developing a hospitality experience that no one else can get, that is memorable and is appealing to the people you want to entertain.

Often the 'money can't buy' experience involves some risk – a concept sponsors find difficult to accept. It might be sponsorship of a new stage show, for example. A great deal of the value comes out of the campaign before the production opens – big advertising campaigns, press campaigns, pre-sale offers to data base, etc. There may be a big party on opening night, or invitations to the sponsor's VIP list, but there is no guarantee the show will be the best show – it may be a disappointment. The 'money can't buy' is a post-show supper on the stage, among the set – a great idea, but access to the stage cannot be facilitated until 45 minutes after the performance finishes – 11.45 p.m.! A young event producer may not be sensitive to the fact that many of the target guests might find the notion of a function commencing this late off-putting. They might choose not to attend, or to attend the performance and decline the function.

Developing the corporate hospitality with the sponsor is the best outcome; they should look after their best interests. They will then judge the success or otherwise from a more realistic and appreciative position.

Ambush marketing

This term refers to the actions of a non-sponsor that imply they have rights to exploit the property (Schlossberg 1996; Howard and Crompton 1995). This is most often seen in sporting events such as the Olympic Games. One of the largest (Mullin 2007) sources of revenue for sport properties comes from the sale of 'official sponsor' rights. Sponsors invest significant amounts of money to secure the rights, typically exclusive within their product or service category, to utilise the property's trademarks in their advertising and promotion campaigns as a means of associating with the property's goodwill. However, marketers working on the properties side of the event industry face challenges that result from a method of marketing called ambush marketing.

Ambush marketing occurs when a company capitalises on the goodwill of an event by using a variety of advertising and promotional tactics to imply an official association with the event. The ambush tactic weakens a competitor's official association with the event acquired by sponsorship.

The issue is that various research studies indicate that ambushing works – and it is very difficult to make sure that it does not happen (Shank 2005). The Olympic Games has probably attracted more attention than other events due to the 'value' associated with the events. Richards (1998, pp 152–153) outlines some examples of ambushing associated with the Olympics such as:

> At the 1992 Barcelona Games, car manufacturer Toyota was an Australian Team sponsor. Without any connection to the Games, Holden offered a golden car to any Australian athlete who won a gold medal. For a fraction of the sponsorship fee paid by Toyota, Holden received significantly greater exposure.

Sporting goods manufacturer Reebok was a sponsor of the 1996 Atlanta Olympic Games. Rival Nike was accused of ambushing the Olympics by:

- purchasing considerable signage around the city of Atlanta;
- building an interactive entertainment complex overlooking the Olympic Park;
- handing out flags and signs to spectators;
- the publicity generated by the gold shoes worn by world record breaking sprinter, Michael Johnson.

Protecting the event

While it is difficult to consider all the potential ways the event can be exploited, if the event warrants it and the stakes are high there are a number of avenues open.

Trademark

Primary among the steps necessary to protect against ambush marketing is to ensure the event producers have effectively protected, usually by trademark registration, the principal visual identifiers of the event, from the names and logos to obligatory mascots and merchandise.

Legislation

In Australia the producers of the Sydney 2000 Olympic Games called on legislation through the Australian Parliament to protect its brand and those of the sponsors and other stakeholders. There were in fact two pieces – the Olympic Insignia Protection Act 1987 (Australian Government 1987) and the Sydney 2000 Games (Indicia and Images) Protection Act 1996 (Australian Government 1996). This Act provided the ownership of these designs and devices to the Australian Olympic Committee. Similar legislative protection was introduced for the London 2012 Games in the form of the London Olympic Games and Paralympic Games Act 2006 and the Olympic Symbol Etc. (Protection) Act 1995.

The first Act protected the various imagery owned by the IOC – the torch, the rings and the motto *citius, altius, fortius* (faster, higher, stronger). This Act prohibits applying the Olympic design or devices on any material; importing into Australia for sale or business any article containing any design; and selling, offering or hiring any article with the Olympic design or devices.

The second Act protected the designs and devices and other intellectual property of the Sydney Games. It was realised that a company could easily imply an association with the Sydney 2000 Olympic Games without using the previously protected designs and devices. The Act prohibited the use of certain words, expressions and images for commercial purposes. These words and expressions included: Games City, Millennium Games, Sydney Games, any combination of 'Games' and '2000' or 'Two Thousand', Olympiad, Olympic, Paralympiad, Paralympic, Share the Spirit, Summer Games, Team Millennium, any combination of the '24th', 'Twenty-fourth' or 'XXIV' and 'Olympics' or 'Games', any combination of '11th', 'Eleventh' or 'XIth' and 'Paralympics' or 'Games', and any combination of a word, phrase or number from List A or List B (see Table 7.1).

Table 7.1 List A and B

List A	List B	List B	List B
Olympian	Bronze	Gold	Green and Gold
Olympics	Games	Medals	Millennium
Paralympian	Silver	Spirit	Sponsor
Paralympics	Summer	Sydney	Two Thousand or 2000

Source: Australian Government 1996.

While the Act specifically describes the designs and devices, the prohibited images are only defined in general terms:

> any visual or aural representations that, to a reasonable person, in the circumstances of the presentation, would suggest a connection with the Sydney 2000 Olympic Games.
>
> (Australian Government 1996, Section 9)

SOCOG (Sydney Organising Committee for the Olympic Games) and SPOC (Sydney Paralympic Organising Committee) were vested as the owners of these words, designs and devices and had the right to profit from licensing these terms. Companies using this material without permission were liable to court action seeking an injunction, corrective advertising or damages against any unauthorised use of the protected material.

In the US (Mullin 2007) ambush marketing can violate Section 43(a) of the Lanham (Trademark) Act (15USC) 1946 as amended in 1988, if they present the false message that a brand owner is an official sponsor or affiliated to them when in fact they are not. This is referred to as 'passing off'. Such conduct can also raise issues of unfair competition, breach of contract, the tort of inference with contractual relations and the tort of inference with prospective business advantage.

In the UK these issues are covered in the Trade Mark Act 1994, but for passing off, usually a common law tort covers the matter, or in more serious cases statutory misrepresentation.

While the Sydney 2000 Olympic legislation was specific to the Olympic Games, similar legislation to that of the US provides a legal remedy where certain instances could conceivably raise questions of prima facie tort and violation of various trading Acts.

Outdoor advertising

One of the common ways to ambush is by purchasing outdoor signage, from big format billboards to taxi advertising. Following the Sydney 2000 Olympic Games, Olympic host city contracts require the host city to control all outdoor advertising sites. This measure was introduced to protect sponsors.

Covering up all brand signs

The Olympic Games are so protective of their brand and the fact that it may be exploited that they cover up brand names on all material used at the venues. For example, brand names that might appear on a toilet are plastered over lest the toilet manufacturer uses an image purporting its product to be 'the throne of the stars'.

Ticketing policies

SOCOG introduced ticketing policies (Washington 1997) to limit the exposure to big blocks of tickets being sold, to prevent ambush by crowd marketing. This is where a block of seats may be occupied by audience members dressed to promote a brand and this block becomes attractive to television coverage, thereby ambushing the event sponsors.

Aerial exclusion zones

Policies were introduced to protect the air space over venues to limit the prospect of skywriting or other airborne ambush.

Broadcast

One of the easiest ways a competitor can ambush is advertising in the broadcast of the event. This can sometimes be negotiated but needs to be controlled by the event producer at the beginning of the contract negotiation process to ensure the event sponsor's interests are considered before those of other prospective advertisers – competitors or not.

Sponsor awareness campaign

While there are many ways outlined above to limit sponsor ambush, it is increasingly complex and the increasing use of digital communications and territories add to this complexity, and there is another important way a sponsor and event producer can protect their investment – use the opportunities to the maximum.

To the event producer – develop a campaign to promote the sponsors and reveal how they have shown the spirit to invest in the event. SOCOG ran a campaign that promoted its sponsors. Below is the copy of one such advertisement:

'It's what dreams are made of'

> Without sponsors, there would be no Olympic Games. Without the Olympic Games, there would be no dreams. Without dreams there would be nothing. Please study this emblem carefully; companies who carry it have committed their support to every Olympic athlete and every Olympic event. They have committed their products, their people, their financial resources and their services, including travel, food and technology, on behalf of every Australian. It's why they have earned the right to the Sydney 2000 Olympic Games emblem.
>
> (SOCOG 1997, pp. 8–9)

To the sponsor – leverage the property, develop a campaign across all media to promote the association and do not rely on the event producer to reinforce your key messages. This is where integrated marketing communications comes into play.

There is an interesting example of an alleged ambush marketing campaign at the Cricket World Cup in South Africa in 2003. Many believe the producers went too far when they had a spectator removed from the stadium – a South African businessman who was found to have been consuming a can of Coca-Cola. The official sponsor was Pepsi-Cola. The businessman accused the producers of assault and took legal action. The negative media coverage that resulted from this incident may not have helped Pepsi's rival but what it did do was indirectly make Pepsi look unreasonable and overly sensitive (Kolah 2003).

Sponsorship management plan

The sales process in securing a sponsor is full of highs and lows; the thrill of securing a new sponsor or signing up a new property is very rewarding.

The next stage is the management of the sponsorship and both parties need their own resources and commitment in order to maximise the benefits the relationship can provide.

> Each sponsorship regardless of its size, requires a sponsorship plan.
> (Skildum-Reid and Grey 2008, p. 157)

Some of this detail will be included in the contract and some may have been discussed in the sales process, but there will be other matters that need to drawn out by both parties.

The sponsor tends to pay for rights, with some low level benefits such as marketing exposure, hospitality and promotional opportunities. These need to be developed and targets or other key performance indicators need to be shared.

It is in both party's interest that the sponsorship works, and defining how this will be measured is key to the project and requires resourcing from both the sponsors and the event. Sometimes there will be assumptions that either party may make about the sponsorship and these assumptions need to be shared and tested. The relative importance of one outcome might be ranked higher by the sponsor than the event producer, for example.

In order to measure results the key performance indicators first need to be established; these need to be clearly measurable indicators, and possibly the measurement needs to begin before the event takes place and then be repeated sometime after the event is completed in order to establish benchmarking of the sponsorship impact.

The sponsorship management plan will be a document that both parties will approve, and it will include the reason why the sponsorship was undertaken, the objectives of the sponsorship, the target markets, the sponsorship benefits, evaluation, action list and budget.

While there is some interest in making the document as brief as possible, it is necessary to include proper details so that the plan can be read and interpreted by other people. As Skildum-Reid (Skildum-Reid and Grey 2008, p. 161) says, 'avoid two word objectives'. The sponsorship objective 'increase sales' is too vague on its own. Does it refer to sales overall, just retail sales or sales in a particular territory, or is it the sales period from the start of the marketing campaign until six months after the event? Two word objectives create more questions than answers.

Maintain long-term relationships between sponsor and the event producer

> It is usually far easier to renew an existing sponsor than it is to find a new one.
> (Skildum-Reid and Grey 2008, p. 186)

The competition for sponsors among event producers seems to increase each year while the measurement and the need to deliver tangible and measurable benefits similarly increases each year.

In a market where supply and demand are out of alignment, i.e. there are more demanding than supplying sponsorship, those with a relationship in place are at an advantage. The sponsorship dollar should never be assumed or underserviced. A good manager or account director needs to understand the personalities and processes of their sponsor's business to ensure the health of the relationship. It would be wrong to assume that the sponsorship funds can be regarded as net income for the event because there are costs attached to the sponsorship such as staff time to manage the relationship and tickets.

In order to achieve this regular meetings are essential, as is record keeping of the meetings. It is important for both parties to appreciate the importance of the relationship and ensure that it is not taken for granted. It is also good strategy for the sponsor to be on the inside of the decision making. The more they feel as if they are part of the establishment, the harder it is to withdraw.

Effective resource management

As the sponsorship programme grows from either the sponsor's or the event's perspective, it can be cost effective to allocate staff to manage and co-ordinate sponsorship activities within the organisation, to co-ordinate the internal use of the sponsorship.

In order to present a fully integrated marketing campaign around the event, internal co-ordination and buy in are essential. This sponsorship co-ordinator will also be required to ensure appropriate budgets are developed and approved to support either the property's investment in the sponsor or the sponsor's investment and leverage funds for the event.

External organisations specialising in sponsorship, such as activation agencies, public relations, marketing or advertising firms, could be used as an alternative to, or in addition to, in-house staff. This can be a means of tapping into a range of people with skills and expertise or getting an informed, external opinion on the value of the event's value to potential sponsors and getting creative advice on sponsors who may have potential synergy with agency programmes and may not have existing sponsorship commitments.

Effective resource management requires both parties to monitor the overall costs and benefits of their sponsorship programme. This should include quantifying the costs associated with attracting and servicing sponsors, the cost to the agency of providing direct benefits to sponsors, and the time spent by sponsorship/development staff, curatorial staff and agency executives. If an agency uses volunteers, the resource implications for their management may also need to be considered.

Case study 7.1

Qantas Australian Grand Prix

Often the outcomes of a sponsorship, as driven and negotiated by the sponsorship and marketing functions, are very focused on return on investment – ROI. Sometimes the outcomes of a sponsorship from other parts of the business differ from those of the sponsorship and marketing functions.

In 2010 Qantas took up the naming rights to the Australian Grand Prix, having previously sponsored the event in a lower capacity. In the post-event report there are substantial details demonstrating that it was a model in terms of integrated marketing communication; the foreword by the Qantas chief executive in the programme outlines his view of the partnership.

> Qantas is proud to be Premier Partner of the 2011 Formula 1™ Qantas Australian Grand Prix again in 2011, marking the second year as Title Sponsor.
>
> In November last year, Qantas celebrated its 90th birthday. And for 25 of those years, Qantas has been supporting this spectacular event, having first joined the Formula 1™ Australian Grand Prix team when it started in Australia in 1985.
>
> Last month, Qantas unveiled its Grand Prix Livery on one of its Boeing 747s. The aircraft is not only testament to the airline's support for Formula One racing, it also promotes the Australian Grand Prix in numerous cities around the world as it embarks on its daily international schedule.
>
> And last year, Qantas added a piece of Hollywood to the Australian Grand Prix. Who could forget the fanfare as Qantas Ambassador-at-Large, John Travolta, visited Albert Park and waved the chequered flag at the end of the race?
>
> This year, Qantas is also directly supporting Australia's home grown sporting great, Mark Webber, and welcomes Mark on board as a Qantas Ambassador. Qantas wishes Mark the best of luck for the pinnacle race on the Grand Prix calendar in Melbourne this year.
>
> Qantas looks forward to flying in fans from around the world to catch all the excitement at the 2011 Formula 1™ Qantas Australian Grand Prix — both on and off the track.
>
> (Alan Joyce, chief executive officer, Qantas Airways)

The report is focused exclusively in the domestic, Australian market, but the chief executive seems to have his vision on the international market.

Vignette

You are approached by a high profile and passionate supporter of jazz music, who is a very wealthy and elderly individual associated with a private manufacturing company. He is known as honourable and trustworthy.

He has heard on the jazz lovers' grapevine that you will be bringing famous jazz musicians to the country for a national tour.

The jazz musicians' management is pressuring for a contract in order to have the certainty of the offer and you believe they are considering other offers, which may lead to them deciding against the tour. A contract will lock in the deal.

The tour's finances involve more risk than you would ordinarily take on, but with the knowledge that there is a prospective sponsor you proceed to negotiate the deal with the musician's agent.

In your projections you have allowed for an income from sponsorship of $200,000 for the two-week tour taking in eight performances which, based on your knowledge and the popularity of the artists, seems to be what the market would bear.

The agent agrees and the contract is duly signed – with reasonably stiff penalty clauses for breaching the contract.

On returning to your office you receive a phone call – from the wife of the high-profile passionate supporter – stating that he died that afternoon.

What recourse do you have and can you rescue the situation?

Summary

This chapter dealt with three major issues: the sponsorship contract, what sponsorship ambush involves, and the sponsorship management plan.

All of these issues are of major consideration in professional sponsorship operations; the degree to which they involve time investment will vary depending on the amount of investment and the value of the assets involved.

Discussion questions

1 How far should an event producer go to protect the sponsor from ambush marketing?
2 Explain the advantages and disadvantages of protecting from ambush.
3 What is the point of a sponsorship management plan?

Bibliography

Australian Government (1987) Olympic Insignia Protection Act 1987. Australian Government, Canberra.
—— (1996) Sydney 2000 Games (Indica and Images) Protection Act 1996 (Cth). Australian Government, Canberra.
British Government (1995) Olympic Symbol Etc. (Protection) Act 1995. British Government, London.
—— (2006) London Olympic Games and Paralympic Games Act 2006. British Government, London.
Geldard, E. and Sinclair, L. (2002) The Sponsorship Manual: Sponsorship Made Easy, The Sponsorship Unit, Upper Ferntree Gully, VIC, Australia.
Howard, D. and Crompton, J. L. (1995) Financing Sport, Fitness Information Technology, Morgantown, WV.
Kolah, A. (2003) Maximising the Value of Sponsorship, Sports Business Group, London.
Mullin, B. H. (2007) Sport Marketing, 3rd edn, Human Kinetics, Champaign, IL.

Richards, C. (1998) *Structuring Effective Sponsorships*, LBC Information Services, Rozelle, NSW, Australia.

Schlossberg, H. (1996) *Sports Marketing*, Cambridge, MA, Blackwell.

Shank, M. D. (2005) *Sports Marketing: A Strategic Perspective*, 3rd edn, Pearson Prentice Hall, Upper Saddle River, NJ.

Skildum-Reid, K. and Grey, A.-M. (2008) *The Sponsorship Seeker's Toolkit*, 3rd edn, McGraw-Hill Australia, Sydney.

SOCOG (1997) *The Australian Financial Review*, Australian Financial Review, Fairfax Media, Sydney, Australia, pp. 8 and 9.

The Lanham (Trademark) Act (Pub.L. 79–489, 60 Stat. 427, enacted July 6, 1946, codified at 15 U.S.C. § 1051 et seq. (15 U.S.C. ch 22)).

Washington, S. (1997) 'Richo has Olympic tickets on himself', *The Australian Financial Review*, 18 December, p. 12.

Measuring ROI
(return on investment)

Learning outcomes

After reading and discussing the contents of this chapter, students will be able to:

- explain the importance of evaluation;
- outline different forms of evaluation;
- detail the meaning of ROI and assumptions involved in measuring it.

Introduction

As sponsorship has been embraced as a tool in the marketing activities of companies and brands, so has the increase in research measuring the impact of sponsorship programmes. The impact of sponsorship has also altered from being about the measurement of logo impressions to deeper measurement of the sponsorship in relation to the specific market segment on which the sponsor wants to make an impression. A demand for financial accountability and budget contestability among the other marketing tools has been the main driver.

Valuing sponsorship

While the landscape of sponsorship continues to change (Howard and Crompton 1995) the director of consumer influence operations at General Motors said 'If cuts in our ad budgets are made, the first thing to go is events sponsorship, because nobody knows what they are getting' (Penzer 1990, p. 162).

'You can't tally up everything on Monday morning and ask if participation in an sports event was successful', said Steven Cross, then corporate event manager at AT&T (*Chicago Tribune* 1990, Mike Meyers, Minneapolis – St Paul Star Tribune, Feb 19).

John Beckthen, pro sports marketing manager at Miller Brewing, stated 'I have yet to see a scientific formula definitely showing sales results from a sporting promotion. A lot of it is gut feel' (*Chicago Tribune* 1990, Mike Meyers, Minneapolis – St Paul Star Tribune, Feb 19).

The research on the effectiveness of sponsorship has evolved over time as techniques have become increasingly sophisticated. Most of the research in the 1980s and 1990s was based on calculating the number of impressions generated, column inches of media or competition entries.

Today, as sponsorship fees (Mullin *et al.* 2007) are under more scrutiny and 'return on investment' and 'activation' and 'leveraging' have become key principles of sponsorship, measurement has become a science and data needs are greater than ever – quantifiable data that can be scrutinised.

As the corporate demand for accountability in marketing expenditure increases, so does the need for a deeper understanding of the unique elements of event sponsorship as a strategic resource and a tool for marketing (Meenaghan 1991; Aguilar-Manjarrez and Kidd 1998).

John Wilkins was head of the sponsorship research unit at Research Surveys in 1995. His department was set up in the early 1980s and has been tracking the success of sports sponsorship since then. Wilkins recalls:

> In the mid-to-late Eighties, most sponsorship was driven by corporate objectives and the sort of research companies were asking for was relatively unsophisticated. They measured success in terms of things like column inches in the press. As time went by, they had to justify their sponsorship budget more and more, and they couldn't simply follow the chairman's whim any longer. Sponsorship is now controlled in most cases by the marketing department, and it is looking for information on how it has reached its target audience, whether by geodemographics, age or behaviour patterns.

> (Croft 1995)

Measuring ROI (return on investment)

Nigel Geach, associate director of the British agency Sports Marketing Surveys, agrees with Wilkins that pressure on budgets, brought about by the recession of the early 1990s, has forced clients to be more responsible and sophisticated about their sponsorship budgets. He says:

> There is increased research into whether sponsorship is delivering. If someone put £X into golf, they want to make sure they are getting through to the right people. A lot of the work we do now is pre-evaluation: looking at events, checking the demographics of the people who watch the sport or participate, and then matching the profile against the target market for the product. More and more, today's sponsorship will have been evaluated in advance.
>
> (Croft 1995)

These results can actually have a significant bearing on the price paid for the rights as a rigorous valuation will result in the 'value' the sponsor might be able to extract from the sponsorship.

> Nevertheless while most evaluate their sponsorship effectiveness many rely on informal measures and assumed benefits for which they have no independent corroboration.
>
> (Gendall 2008, p. 284)

Geldard and Sinclair (2002) identify three reasons why evaluation is critical:

- To determine whether planned sponsorship (marketing and communications) objectives were achieved.
- To determine whether the return on sponsorship investment was worthwhile in comparison to other marketing and communications activities such as conventional advertising and consumer promotions.
- To help improve management and the outcome of the company's overall sponsorship programmes.

IEG claim that the global brands are using tools to measure sponsorship impact to test across the spectrum of sponsorships – from local events to global events and from five-figure deals to eight-figure deals. They believe this is the start of a trend as accountability needs to be justified more and more. A study by IBM in October 2011 of chief marketing officers (CMOs) found nearly two thirds felt ROI – the direct impact of expenditures on business results – will be the primary measure of marketing effectiveness by 2015 (IEG Consulting 2012).

One of the challenges in measuring sponsorship and impact is that with the appropriate 360 degree 'detonation', there is a great deal of data to collect and analyse. IEG stated:

> measuring multifaceted engagement rather than one dimensional reach and evaluating the complex eco-system of sponsorship – with its ability to impact multiple audiences – requires at least the same amount of data, rigor and analysis that is used to access the tools in the marketing arsenal.
>
> (IEG Consulting 2012, p. 3)

Timing

It is important in any research to consider three phases:

- before event
- during event
- post event.

One of the major indicators will be the change of awareness as the campaign and other activities are taking place. Therefore it is important to undertake some baseline research – research before the sponsorship activity takes place. Furthermore, some goals or KPIs (key performance indicators) as to the effectiveness of the marketing/sponsorship awareness campaign are to be set. This is sometimes referred to as 'benchmarking'.

Nigel Geach stressed that sponsorship no longer exists in a vacuum – at least, with the more sophisticated users. It will be integrated with the rest of the marketing mix. He asks, 'If Carling puts £Xm into sponsorship, how much more will it spend on tied-in promotions?'

This point is endorsed by Matthew Patten, client services director of sponsorship consultancy Orbit International. In his opinion,

> Certainly the top FMCG companies are much more sophisticated about use of sponsorship. They have a long-term view: it has to have a strategic rationale. It has to be extendible into other areas of the marketing mix, because they will be using it to drive other activities such as direct marketing, sales promotion and above-the-line advertising. They are even looking at how it fits in with interactive media.
>
> (Croft 1995)

Patten claims that if the clients are not using sophisticated research techniques, such as Mosaic profiling or lifestyle data bases, to analyse their sponsorship, then the sponsorship consultancies are. He says 'there's much more of a planning function, in the advertising agency sense, to sponsorship these days'.

So it is important to consider the markets that the sponsor is trying to reach – for a broad based consumer good the market might be to the entire population but for young home buyers such a broad awareness might not be the most effective way to make a connection.

Sponsorship management plan

In Chapter 6 we referred to the sponsorship management plan, a document that brings all the elements of the sponsorship together. Strangely it does not focus on the event but on the sponsorship and how the sponsor will extract the anticipated value from the relationship.

Along with the budget for the sponsorship, leverage activities including hospitality, signage, advertising, printing, photography, etc., there need to be allowances for research. This may include media monitoring, online and face-to-face questionnaires.

This plan will ensure that the research that is collected is relevant and useful and can be justified or not as a worthwhile element of the sponsor's ongoing business activity.

This plan will embrace internal and external drivers as well as consumer and business channel partners, government and regulatory stakeholder relations and other elements. These all have a bearing on the value of the partnership and were most likely considered in the decision making in taking up the sponsorship. They may have been secondary in the decision making; but in the sponsorship management plan they need to be weighted accordingly in the evaluation.

Investment

Sometimes it seems that more money is spent supporting and justifying a sponsorship than the fees paid for the rights involved in taking on the sponsorship. It is therefore important to consider all the associated costs in the initial decision making process. What is to be achieved in the process of the sponsorship?

Event producers undertake research themselves; can all the parties therefore combine to undertake one major piece of research considering the multiple outcomes of awareness, attitude and demographics?

All parties associated with the event will be interested in evaluation of the event in different ways and in some cases the more the event producer can be engaged in bringing it all together the better. Not all the research is likely to be positive. Meenaghan (1991) provides guidance for future sponsorships – maximising what went right and learning from mistakes rather than repeating them.

Sometimes the various parties forget that at the end of the day the audience or consumers may tire of being questioned by multiple interest groups, and so the audience's patience needs to be considered in the process as well. Overdone or unsophisticated sponsorship can lead to negative public reactions and over-researched consumers can respond negatively to questionnaires.

Measurement

Just as each sponsorship management plan differs, so too do the ways in which they are measured. There are no industry standards as there may be in television or other traditional media in relation to advertising sales. Meenaghan (1991) identifies three main methods used.

Sales effectiveness

Judging the success of a sponsorship for sales represents the most basic outcome of marketing driven activity, and so it is not surprising that sponsors view the success or otherwise of the sponsorship as based on impact on sales performance. The issue is time frame and leverage activity. Will the sales be measured incrementally from a baseline set pre-marketing campaign? Will there be any additional incentives for the purchase of the product, like a promotional giveaway or competition for consumers? It is unlikely that there would be any impact if there was no incentive to the consumer.

Of course there are sales attributed to the venue, but only if these rights can be seen as separate. In fact there are odd events where a competition, for example, the Rugby Union competition in the Southern Hemisphere, Super 15 Rugby, sponsored by one beer brand – Lion, uses venues for some of the matches that have an exclusive pourage deal with their competition, Fosters. The only exception is in the private suites where the Lion executives can entertain their channel partners with their own product rather than have to consider sampling their opponent's.

Of course this might be harder to judge if the sponsor was not in the business of sales – for example, the sponsorship by a building firm may be intended to lift brand awareness and build a contact base for sales that may come into fruition many years after the event.

Media exposure

One of the simplest methods is to measure the amount of media coverage the event attracts. This tends to be valued on what it would cost if it was purchased – and then rounded down depending on content. For example, if the article has no reference to the sponsor its value is scaled down, but if there is a front page photo story in colour with the logo clearly on view its value is scaled up.

Communication effectiveness

While the first two relied on secondary data – sales figures and media coverage – this method relies on getting direct feedback from the end user, the consumer. This measure is designed to allow for the evaluation of the cognitive effects – the mental process effects – of the sponsorship. It measures attitude change – how the sponsor regards being seen connected to a particular event. There are two particular techniques which seem to be most prevalent based on literature (McDonald 1991; Parker 1991). They are to research continuously or intermittently. These two distinct methods obviously vary in the frequency of the research, but also in the specific questions being asked.

This research can be undertaken in relation to the general population by random methods such as telephone surveys or in relation to a targeted audience such as those who purchased tickets or registered for the event, or members of the club. It might involve some form of competition, soliciting entries during an online broadcast to members or another method such as use of social media. The results will differ widely; nevertheless, it all comes back to the leverage plans, the scale of the investment and the nature of the sponsor's business.

Similarly results will vary greatly depending on whether respondents are prompted or unprompted in their questions regarding awareness of sponsors. It is suggested (Tripodi 2003) that the concept of prompted awareness compromises the process of sponsorship. Rossiter and Percy's (1997) and others' (Cornwell and Maignan 1998; Quester and Farrelly 1998) stance from a methodological perspective was that it was not correct to use the event as a cue to ask the subjects which companies or brands sponsored the event. They argue that this is not, as mentioned above, representative of the real world where the 'choice situation dictates consumer focus upon the brand rather than the event' (Rossiter and Percy 1997, p. 442). They propose an alternative methodology which leads in a different way with questioning along the lines of 'when you think of Company X, what sponsorships come to mind?' Again it is important to consider the market sample as if it is a localised sponsorship activity; a countrywide survey will not perhaps be in the interests of the sponsor or the event producer because the results might be too small for proper analysis. This brings us back to the sponsorship management plan, where these definitions of markets to influence and therefore to research, will be outlined.

- *Measurement methods*: sales as a measurement tool need to consider on multiple levels as Skildum-Reid proposes (Skildum-Reid and Grey 2008).
- *New customers*: customers that have not previously purchased the product or services before being enticed due to the sponsorship.
- *Loyalty*: existing customers that may be enticed to remain loyal due to the sponsorship; whether by way of inducement or because of the sponsor's commitment to the event or cause.
- *Incremental sales*: customers enticed to purchase a greater quantity of the sponsor's product as a result of the sponsorship.
- *Upselling*: while similar to the incremental sales it involves the purchase of ancillary products like an extended warranty for an electronic good or a sunroof for a car that is not part of the package.

Each of these is important in the sales matrix; but each needs to be considered separately in the analysis.

Therefore measuring ROI or sponsorship evaluation needs to be considered in the process of deciding on the sponsorship. It needs to be focused and targeted before the decision to take up the sponsorship. Sponsorships are increasingly more heavily scrutinised, and an event promoter is in an increasingly competitive world for sponsors. It is more in the event promoter's interests to understand in advance what outcomes the sponsor is looking for and to interrogate this in advance so strategies can be put in place to maximise these returns, and to integrate these activities as far as possible in the event marketing, hospitality and other associated activities.

Sponsorship evaluation services

As the demands on sponsors become more contestable and the outcomes of sponsorships more exacting, firms have emerged with various tools to assist in the decision making surrounding sponsorship proposals.

Major firms are approached by event promoters with opportunities, some fantastically targeted and others random approaches. Evaluation of these approaches is very difficult and time consuming.

Event producers would have noticed the increasing use by major sponsors of online applications – these have been designed to make the job of evaluation easier. It is less about the beautiful documentation and more about the facts. The right software application can stack the entire proposal against others and cause a tactical rather than emotional response. It removes or quarantines the decision maker's influence and focuses instead on the predetermined outcomes of the sponsorship.

Interestingly, these services also provide a benchmarking service which helps the sponsor understand the state of the market for similar opportunities providing insights into industry standards and expectations. There are a number of firms focused on this market. One company is Sponsorium.

Sponsorium has built its intelligence from thousands of sponsorship opportunities across more than 35 countries, and measured against the sponsorship criteria of a variety of brands.

Subscribers are provided with a report including:

- An industry score and index on how sponsorship proposals meet the needs of brands.
- What the brands are looking for and how rights owners can improve their offering.
- The average annual rights fee and how it differs by Sector.
- The cost effectiveness of sponsorship and how each Sector compares.

The report is written for a wide market – Whether you are a Sponsor, Rights Owner or a Government Department, the SPONSORIUM Report will provide you with a better understanding of the industry, how you can improve performance and ultimately increase your share of the marketing budget.

The annual SPONSORIUM Report comes in with updates on all trends and special reports on individual Sectors covering: Arts, Consumer Shows, Community, Festivals & Fairs, Ethnic events, Education, Government Relations, Leisure, Media, Music, Sports, Tourism, Trade Shows & Exhibitions.

(*Sponsorium Report* n.d.)

There are many other firms offering evaluation, such as Repucom, who have specialised in evaluating sponsorship involving media exposure such as televised sports:

There is an increased need for accountability in all types of marketing. Television advertising uses ratings and print media uses readership surveys amongst other things to make decisions on the allocation of marketing spend. However, the value of other marketing levers, like branded content and sponsorships, has long been a contentious issue argued by sponsors, rights holders, broadcasters, advertisers and media buyers.

Repucom provides a new level of evidence based accountability for branded content and sponsorship by offering an irrefutable means of quantifying brand exposure in broadcast. In addition to this, Repucom supports brand exposure quantification with both customised and bespoke effectiveness research and a commitment to providing its clients with industry-leading insights and recommendations to maximise their marketing investment. Repucom also aims to generate regular industry reports, with a goal of providing benchmarking and insight across common industry issues.

(Repucom 2012)

Case study 8.1

'AT&T makes the call'

Telecommunications giant AT&T, one of the largest and best known US media spenders, activates nearly 150 corporate partnerships plus over 200 more local and regional ones. These properties range from the US Olympic team to sporting and performing arts venues, to collegiate institutions and more. Many of these partnerships come with complex assets that must be managed by the company's corporate sponsorship team.

Objective

AT&T sought to create a centralised tracking system to organise their portfolio of sponsorships and events. The corporate team, along with multiple agency partners and eventually regional marketing managers, needed to be able to communicate more efficiently and effectively having access to up-to-date information whenever they need it. Beyond allowing for tracking and information sharing, AT&T also needed to analyse their findings.

From a structure standpoint, AT&T manages the portfolio by breaking it into five regions, including many personnel working in markets outside of corporate HQ in Dallas.

Opportunity

The data that AT&T sought to centralise was residing within contracts, spreadsheets and emails, which existed and were shared among team members and with properties. Upon enlisting PerforMind, the team worked to extract the figures and entitlements that they owned with each property.

Many of AT&T's partnerships are multi-year and as a result budget information surrounding rights fees, in-kind and activation costs is equally complex. Beyond the assets, entitlements and financials, each partnership comes with extensive files relating to breathing life into it through engagement. AT&T's corporate, regional and agency teams all collaborate to deliver a finished product. This includes site layouts, logos and calendaring that constantly posed a problem.

Lastly, as a national sponsor, AT&T received thousands of proposals per year. Support teams spent countless hours reviewing proposals that they received through a web site, but the opportunity to merge the tracking of these proposals, apply their specific criteria to them and have their existing partnership data in one place proved extremely useful.

Outcome

Success for AT&T and its use of PerforMind can be measured for efficiency. What previously took extensive communication outreach to ensure accuracy of data (among internal corporate and regional teams, properties and agencies), now takes seconds as their tool has become their source for everything concerning sponsorship in the company.

AT&T's associate director for corporate sponsorships, Danielle Kent, has recognised two impactful results: 'Efficiency. The tool has allowed us to take the breadth of our data and centralize it in one easy to access and easy to manage location.' She continues: 'Secondly the greatest experience we've had is being able to apply rigorous measurement and establish measurable goals in terms of managing our sponsorship portfolio.'

Below is a breakdown of system use:

- 300+ partnerships;
- 5 distinct sponsorship regions;
- 60+ users across AT&T and agency teams.

Upon testing some weighted criteria within PerforMind, assistant vice president for events and sponsorship, Jason Simpson, saw yet another angle related to the justification of strategy and budget: 'This is really impressive. It allows us to tell our story.'

Source: PerforMind provided this case study after discussion with their client AT&T

Summary

The evaluation of sponsorship is an increasingly important dimension of the sponsorship process. If your event is ongoing, rather than one-off, the importance of keeping sponsors and not having to find new ones each time, each season, is key. In order to keep sponsors committed it is essential to ensure efforts are directed in considering the sponsor's aims in the partnership and addressing them.

Discussion questions

1 Discuss the different forms of evaluation.
2 What are the benefits of using an external party to undertake the evaluation of a sponsorship?
3 Why is timing of the evaluation so important?

References

Aguilar-Manjarrez, R. and Kidd, C. (1998) 'Sports sponsorship development in leading Canadian companies: Issues and trends', *International Journal of Advertising*, vol. 17, issue 1, pp. 29–49.

Chicago Tribune (1990) 'Corporate sponsors are asking the score', Mike Meyers, Minneapolis – St Paul Star Tribue, 19 February.

Cornwell, T. B. and Maignan, I. (1998) 'An international review of sponsorship research', *Journal of Advertising*, vol. 27, no. 1, pp. 1–21.

Croft, M. (1995) 'Question of sport', *Marketing Week*, 31 March. www.marketingweek.co.uk

Geldard, E. and Sinclair, L. (2002) *The Sponsorship Manual: Sponsorship Made Easy*, The Sponsorship Unit, Upper Ferntree Gully, VIC, Australia.

Gendall, P. (2008) 'An analysis of consumers responses to cause related marketing', *International Journal of Non Profit and Public Sector Marketing*, vol. 20, no. 2, pp. 283–297.

Howard, D. and Crompton, J. L. (1995) *Financing Sport*, Fitness Information Technology, Morgantown, WV.

IEG Consulting (2012) *A Sponsorship Measurement Solution*, IEG, Chicago.

McDonald, C. (1991) 'Sponsorship and the image of the sponsor', *European Journal of Marketing*, vol. 25, no. 11, pp. 31–38.

Meenaghan, T. (1991) 'The role of sponsorship in the marketing communications mix', *International Journal of Advertising*, vol. 10, no. 1, pp. 35–47.

Mullin, B. H., Hardy, S. and Sutton, W. A. (2007) *Sport Marketing*, 3rd edn, Human Kinetics, Champaign, IL.

Parker, K. (1991) 'Sponsorship: The research contribution', *European Journal of Marketing*, vol. 25, no. 11, pp. 22–30.

Penzer, E. (1990) 'How do sponsors gauge the payoffs from event marketing?' *Incentive*, October, pp. 162–164.

Quester, P. and Farrelly, F. (1998) 'Brand association and memory decay effects for sponsorship: The case of the Australian Formula One Grand Prix', *The Journal of Product and Brand Management*, vol. 7, no. 6, pp. 539–556.

Repucom (2012) *What we do*, www.repucom.net/what_we_do.htm (retrieved 20 June 2012 from www.repucom.net).

Rossiter, J. and Percy, L. (1997) *Advertising Communications and Promotion Management*, 2nd edn, McGraw-Hill, New York.

Skildum-Reid, K. and Grey, A.-M. (2008) *The Sponsorship Seeker's Toolkit*, 3rd edn, McGraw-Hill Australia, North Ryde, NSW.

Sponsorium Report: Sponsorship Proposal Managment Software (n.d.) Retrieved 5 June 2012 from www.sponsors.com/en/services/sponsorium-report

Tripodi, M. H. (2003) 'Cognitive evaluation: Prompts used to measure sponsorship awareness', *International Journal of Market Research*, vol. 45, no. 4, pp. 435–455.

Chapter 9

Alternatives to sponsorship

Learning outcomes

After reading and discussing the contents of this chapter, students will be able to:

- list three alternative sources of income outside of traditional sponsorship;
- outline different forms of revenue generation;
- detail the motivations behind each of these alternative funding sources.

Introduction

It is always important to consider all potential revenue streams as income. Each event will have its own unique opportunities and some might involve 'sponsorship', but others might involve alternative income generation associated with other types of activities – these might be related to the event or cause. This essentially is an outcome of the event audit – one of the key resources the event producer has is the audience of the event. How else can the audience be engaged, what opportunities might another group offer that would result in revenue to the event?

Revenue sources

FMCG companies find *sampling* a very powerful way of connecting with a particular audience. They pay reasonable amounts to property owners for this opportunity. If the event was the right scale and had the right positioning, right location and right audience, sampling might be a valid revenue opportunity. It is often felt that consumers are unlikely to change purchasing decisions for certain product categories based on advertising alone. For example, toothpaste is a product where there is a tendency to purchase the same brand over a long term and in order to change behaviour it would involve providing a trial product, a sample, in order for someone to consider changing allegiance.

Another revenue opportunity is the *catering* – both food and beverages. This might be impacted by the sampling; however, there is obviously revenue to be potentially made on the turnover. Additionally it may be a requirement from an FMCG category sponsor that their products are on sale, providing both an income from the brand association, the sales rights and the retail margin or commission depending on whether the retail side is being managed internally or externally. In some cases, venues will already have exclusive relationships with suppliers and not be able to accommodate specific brands in their offerings due to other relationships.

One example of this conflict is beer. Often in Australia a venue will have a pourage or sales relationship with one or other of the main beer brands in Australia. This is restricted and pretty watertight in terms of exclusive sales. It does not provide for brand exposure except on equipment and for the purposes of the public awareness of the offering. When an event is sponsored by a competitor or where a team in the competition is sponsored by a competitor of the beer for sale in the venue, it is confusing for the audience. For example, Fosters have exclusive rights to the sales, and Lion Nathan has branding rights to the venue and one of the teams participating. Who wins? Most likely they cancel each other out – however, Lion Nathan gets the television audience and Fosters get the on-premise sales.

Money can be made on selling the rights to be exclusive – an income from the caterer that is guaranteed and also generated on the sales.

Sometimes things can go wrong! McDonalds is a TOP (The Olympic Partner) sponsor of the International Olympic Committee (IOC). Their sponsorship category extended to hot potato chips and French fries and extended over the 800 food retailers at 40 Olympic Games sites in London (news.com.au 2012). There was an exception to the rule, which was when the chips were served with fish for cultural reasons. So other than people purchasing fish and chips, the only venues to sell chips or French fries were the McDonalds venues.

But the London Organising Committee for the Olympic Games (LOCOG) reversed this condition after feedback from caterers who were on the receiving end of abuse from outraged staff working at the opening and closing ceremonies rehearsals and who demanded an end to the chip ban. A sign in a catering area in the Olympic Park stated:

> Please understand this is not the decision of the staff who are serving up your meals who, given the choice, would gladly give it to you, however, they are not allowed to. Please do not give the staff grief; this will only lead to us removing fish and chips completely.

An LOCOG spokesman confirmed that the 'dictatorchip' had been toppled and that chips could now be served alongside chicken, pies or even on their own. 'It's sorted,' he said. 'We have spoken to McDonald's about it' (Carne 2012).

Merchandise

The potential revenue streams depend on the characteristics of the event, timing, scale, audience, uniqueness, tribalism, etc. The following case study demonstrates that in the right circumstances merchandise can be a very significant revenue stream.

Case study 9.1

World Youth Day

World Youth Day is a youth festival for young Catholics held every four years. The 23rd Youth Day was held in Sydney, Australia in and ran for five days from 15 July 2008.

About 500,000 young people from 200 countries attended during the week and many more came for the weekend. They were joined by about 600 bishops and cardinals, as well as by 6,600 reporters from across the world.

The event producers commissioned experienced personnel to manage the merchandising programme. While there was no profit incentive behind the programme, there was a sense of occasion and souvenir/memento driving the programme. The merchandising team were very highly skilled, having worked on many major events and brand building campaigns and were quick to see the potential in such a large gathering and a once-in-a-lifetime experience for most participants.

They worked with the event producers in building a brand and worked with manufacturers and retailers in relation to licensing the brand, thereby maximising distribution and minimising the risk. They used merchandise to build awareness in the general community and built desire for the brand.

Instead of merchandise being positioned as a tack-on activity, they seamlessly connected it to being part of the celebration – and the sales were phenomenal.

There were eight themes of merchandise, the above two giving the impression that the themes were applied to a wide range of souvenirs; the other categories were Australiana, Australian Indigenous, International, Pilgrim, Youth and Religious.

Broadcast and content

Often in developing a property, or event or cause, a wise producer will look at ways in which the asset can be developed in order to increase its value, its reach and its impact. This might have direct financial implications by way of selling exclusive access to content, but it might also be used to simply provide more value to sponsors as a guaranteed exposure.

In today's expanding online world content is everywhere and quality is questionable; but in terms of expanding the exposure of the event and audience transmission of content it can be very significant.

It might be that by securing a media partnership such as a newspaper partnership, the event has a greater asset to secure other partners.

Corporate hospitality

Essentially corporate hospitality is the packaging of exclusive elements to which businesses invite guests in order to entertain them. It is ideal for getting to know prospective clients since it provides a social work setting to build a shared experience, and is useful in enabling parties to move forward on a business proposition as it can provide a less guarded environment. A visible example is corporate boxes in sporting arenas.

To the event producer it can provide a major revenue stream if the event is of interest to the corporate market, and if the facilities required can be sourced at prices that can make the experience a net revenue opportunity with minimal risk.

Corporate hospitality is a global industry estimated to be worth around US$15 billion annually (Blackshaw 2012) for sports alone. When the amount spent on theatre, musicals, concerts and other forms of corporate hospitality is added it is clear that a lot of money is spent in this area. Many major sporting and entertainment venues invest significantly in facilities for corporates to entertain in a manner that makes the guest seem special and the host seem generous.

Blackshaw recognises that the income from corporate hospitality – i.e. where there is no intellectual property involved but simply tickets, access to special spaces, catering and associated benefits to the host and guests – is a significant element in the bottom line of many sports event producers who offer a wide range of commercial rights and packages.

It seems that corporate hospitality, unlike corporate sponsorship, was more resilient in face of the recent global financial downturn. Corporate hospitality is used by companies for a variety of corporate purposes such as entertaining guests or rewarding staff.

Corporate hospitality is not new; but the growth in the number of events does not seem to have dampened the demand for high level entertaining. While it may not be 'money can't buy' in that there can be a number of corporate facilities at an event, therefore, it is not unique, it is does offer the 'look at me' high level networking opportunity that may not be available at some smaller unique events.

Whether corporate hospitality is an effective form of marketing is debatable. Roger Bennett's study (2003, p. 229) identifies four distinct motivations for corporate hospitality:

- Warriors – used strategically and effectively.
- Pragmatists – analysed as being a useful opportunity.
- Reactors – because competitors use corporate hospitality.
- Strategic hopefuls – used from time to time rather than ongoing.

Government grants

Depending on the type of activity and the organisation producing it, there may be government sources that can be considered. They might not be for the whole activity but a particular element of it.

For example, in many Western jurisdictions there are incentives and grants associated with sustainability and the desire to develop showcasing opportunities for good practice. Government funding is sometimes not evident; for example, the Olympic Games, which are often seen as being most significantly funded by corporate sponsorship, but in fact are more often funded principally by the national or provincial governments which host the event.

Government funding can also be attracted to events that provide significant economic impact to an economy. One great example of this is the Monsoon Cup in Malaysia.

Case study 9.2

Monsoon Cup

PulauDuyong had never been known as a tourist destination. It was not as popular as the nearby islands that tourists frequented. It was an ordinary island that had been inhabited by fishermen for generations. It was known as the centre of Islamic civilisation and where the boat building industry started for the locals at one time. PulauDuyong had never been anything more.

Kuala Terengganu is strategically positioned along the South China Sea as a port of call for cruising boats from Northeast Asia to South Asia and Australasia. The current marina at PulauDuyong, Kuala Terengganu, is the only operating mainland marina on the east coast of the Malaysian peninsular.

In July 2005 the prime minister of Malaysia, Tun Abdullah Ahmad Badawi, set foot on the island and PulauDuyong changed forever. Tun Abdullah envisioned a bright future for the island. The Monsoon Cup was born. The Monsoon Cup was an integral part of the prime minister's vision to develop the state of Terengganu.

This prestigious international regatta was to serve as a catalyst for sustainable development of the economy through the positioning of PulauDuyong as a maritime hub for pleasure boating, boat building, boat maintenance and ultimately a marine and sports tourism destination. Moreover, the setting up of the Terengganu Sailing and Maritime Academy enabled the development of local talent through knowledge transfer generated via the event.

The Monsoon Cup has not only catapulted sailing into the Malaysian mindset but is also the catalyst in promoting Terengganu, both as a tourist destination and in developing marine-based business activities. Economic opportunities in the services and manufacturing sectors flourished as well. Among them are hotels, tourism, restaurants, boat building, food supplies, textiles and souvenirs. The Monsoon season that was once seen as a threat is now widely viewed as a business opportunity by the locals.

The Monsoon Cup is a leg of the World Match Race Sailing Tour (WMRT). The Monsoon Cup has also brought some of the world's most famous people together.

The lure of this prestigious event has had celebrities, royalty and VIPs all gracing the shores of PulauDuyong. Many have gone back mesmerised by the sheer magnitude and charisma of the Monsoon Cup. PulauDuyong has morphed from a small quiet fishing island in Terengganu to a world-class host to Malaysia's second biggest sporting event.

Source: Brand Advantage, Sydney, May 2012

Advertising sales

There are often elements of activities that can provide opportunities for advertising sales; for example, these might be printed souvenir programmes, signage at the event, branding on web sites or other marketing driven functions. It is important to ensure that these do not become sponsorships in so far as no intellectual property (IP) or association outside the advertising contract is allowed or otherwise it becomes a sponsorship and could 'white ant' or erode the sponsorships in place.

The Sydney Festival subcontracted the production and publishing of souvenir programmes to a specialist publisher, Playbill. Playbill in turn had the rights to sell advertising in categories where the Festival did not have a sponsor. Indeed they approached all sponsors offering the opportunity to advertise and in most cases this did not take up the full inventory of available space. They then targeted businesses with whom they had ongoing relationships outside the exclusion area. There were a number of cases where it was hard not to think that the associated IP was not being used to bring in the advertiser at an advertising rather than sponsorship rate, sponsorship being higher priced than straight advertising.

Fundraising

The term 'fundraising' means different things in different industries. In the world of banking, fundraising is a commercial activity seeking funding at commercial returns for activities, whereas in the arts, community and non-profit areas it refers to seeking funds for public good. This can range from a sausage sizzle to a second hand book sale – they rely significantly on volunteers and on the community.

In Australia, chocolate manufacturer Cadbury has made a valuable contribution to this category by providing fundraising packages to community organisations to raise money for their cause. These not only present the brand Cadbury as being associated with wide ranging community fundraising but also enable it to sell key products in its portfolio.

The following are examples of feedback from users of Cadbury's fundraising products.

Logan Youth Music Exchange

The Logan Youth Music Exchange (in Brisbane, Australia) was formed in 2001 to give Logan City's best young musicians the opportunity to spread their wings and develop their music. The exchange has built strong relationships with Logan's sister cities and regularly hosts their music groups.

In September 2011, 32 young musicians will tour sister city Hirakata in Japan and perform with local schools, bands and orchestras.

The exchange has worked with Penny and her crew at Cadbury Fundraiser in Brisbane to raise over $12,000 (AU$) to help the musicians on what will be a cultural and musical trip of a lifetime.

(Fundraising Manager)

'Walk on Water'

We formed fundraising group Walk on Water (WOW) after visiting Cambodia in 2009 and being inspired to help underprivileged communities. Through selling Cadbury Fundraiser each week, we get our story out to many corporates. We've raised money to buy rice and medical supplies, and fund learning programs for the New Hope Centre in Siem Reap every month. Our efforts make a significant difference and we sincerely thank Cadbury for opening the doors and making fundraising so easy

(The WOW gals – Walk on Water – Cathy, Louise, Moira and Ruth [Cadbury Australia])

Philanthropy

Philanthropy differs from fundraising in that there is no exchange of benefits. The motivation is not to get a chocolate bar but is driven by the higher purposes of giving back to the community or to the specific cause or endeavour.

The meaning of 'philanthropy' is the sense of caring for, supporting, developing or enhancing humanity and related worldly causes. Fundamentally it is private initiatives for public good, focusing on the quality of life. This formulation distinguishes it from business (private initiatives for private good, focusing on material prosperity such as sponsorship, cause-related marketing or other activities where there is an outcome favourable to the support other than the sense of satisfaction or duty done) and government (public initiatives for public good, focusing on law and order).

There are a number of forms philanthropy can take. Nevertheless, while the motivation for philanthropy is principally altruistic, different jurisdictions incentivise donations by way of tax concessions.

Philanthropy does not usually take place in for-profit enterprises, but in the non-profit enterprise area it is a significant and growing source of funding.

There are three different philanthropic sources:

● individuals;
● foundations and other organisations with the purpose of distributing funds;
● corporations with a commitment to invest in their community.

Each source requires different strategies and techniques; each requires varying degrees of engagement and reporting. This is also relative to the scale of the support and whether it is proposed that the support be ongoing or one-off.

> ### Case study 9.3
>
> ## Sydney Festival 2012: I Am Eora (I Am of this Place)
>
> Lindy Hume, the festival director, had an ambitious plan to present a large scale new commission of a work which told the story of three legends of indigenous Australia – specifically Sydney and the land of the Gadigal people at the time of European settlement, in one epic story. At the centre of the work are three heroes of Aboriginal Sydney whose enduring spirits still inspire: the protest and resistance of the warrior Pemulwuy; the female embodiment of resilience, Barangaroo; and her controversial husband Bennelong, the gifted interpreter who sought reconciliation.
>
> The production involved 50 Aboriginal musicians, performers, creative artists and technicians from across the country who came together for one of the most thrilling and ambitious collaborations ever commissioned by Sydney Festival.
>
> It seems the alternative word for ambitious is costly, and this project required $300,000. Without this injection of funds the production would not be realised and this reality became more real as it was May 2011 and significant work was needed to commence in order for the production to premier in the annual January festival. The Australian financial year begins 1 July and ends 30 June and therefore campaigns for individual support tend to be scheduled to take advantage of this, with campaigns held in May and June.
>
> Sydney Festival had done little work in the philanthropic area previously; nevertheless, with one simple email to the 100 most significant ticket buyers the money started coming in. The Festival had created a category of supporters called 'associate producers', and the name may imply that the role had influence but this was not the case. Each associate producer provided $5,000 (or more in some cases) and they were motivated in supporting the Festival and a project that was widely recognised as being of significant cultural importance. The funds were tax deductible as no tangible benefit was provided in return for the funds; however, the associate producers were acknowledged in a number of ways, given the opportunity to meet the artistes, and to feel they were a part of the creation of this particular work.

Bequests and planned giving

Essentially a 'bequest' is a systematic effort to identify and cultivate a person for the purpose of generating a major gift that is structured and that integrates sound personal, financial and estate-planning concepts with the prospect's plans for lifetime or testamentary giving. A planned gift has tax implications and is often transmitted through a legal instrument, such as a will or a trust. This does differ from country to country as tax laws differ.

In a nutshell, 'planned giving' is the solicitation of major gifts for a non-profit, often contributed by an individual donor through a will, bequest or trust.

Sound management, sources of revenue, especially during difficult economic times, and planned giving can play an important part in a non-profit's overall fundraising plan. Major gifts often make up the top 10–20 per cent of gifts received by an organisation and may account for as much as 70–80 per cent of its overall fundraising revenue, according to Dove (2002). Thus, planned giving can play an important part in diversifying an event producers' source of income and ensuring its long-term financial health.

What constitutes a 'major gift' will vary from one organization to another – a large non-profit may consider a major gift to be a donation of $100,000 or more, while a small start-up may consider $1,000 and above to be a major gift. They do not have to be made with cash or as outright gifts. The gift can be structured over a period of time or can be deferred, and it can involve a variety of assets, including stock, securities and property as well as cash.

These sorts of funds tend not to be directed to events specifically but to elements such as skill development, accessibility and programmes of social inclusion.

Cause-related marketing

Cause-related marketing (CRM) is a mutually beneficial collaboration between a corporation and a non-profit in which their respective assets are combined to:

- create shareholder and social value;
- connect with a range of constituents (be they consumers, employees or suppliers);
- communicate the shared values of both organisations.

American Express first used the phrase 'cause-related marketing' in 1983 to describe its campaign to raise money for the Statue of Liberty's restoration. American Express donated one cent to the restoration every time someone used its charge card. As a result, the number of new cardholders grew by 45 per cent and card usage increased by 28 per cent.

Other examples of cause-related marketing programmes include:

- requests for small donations for children's charities at the supermarket checkout;
- public awareness campaigns for HIV/AIDS, breast cancer and other causes;
- licensing of well-known charity trademarks and logos, like the World Wildlife Fund's panda.

CRM is distinct from corporate philanthropy because the corporate dollars involved in CRM are not outright gifts to a non-profit organisation, so they are not treated as tax-deductible charitable contributions. Non-profits potentially benefit from increased fundraising and exposure. Likewise, corporations that are socially involved potentially benefit from increased brand loyalty and employee morale. Studies have shown that for products of similar quality, consumers will consider the company's image and reputation when choosing a brand. To find and develop CRM opportunities, non-profit organisations should expand their research efforts beyond the traditional corporate giving directories and refer to resources in the business departments of public and/or academic libraries.

There are more details on cause related marketing in Chapter 10.

Philanthrocapitalism

'Philanthrocapitalism' is often defined as the practice of applying business methods and measures to philanthropy, or harnessing the power of the market to achieve the goals of social change. It is seen as partly championed by those who have made large fortunes in the financial markets. Philanthrocapitalists often expect financial or business returns over the long term or secondary benefits from their investment in social programmes.

Philanthrocapitalism is closely aligned to 'venture philanthropy', which is the application of venture capital principles and practices, such as long-term investment and capacity building, to not-for-profit organisations. Venture philanthropy assists non-profit organisations in the plan, launch and management of new programmes or social purpose enterprises.

Finally sponsorship again

Case study 9.4

The Glenmorangie Company

The Glenmorangie Company, distillers of one of the world's most highly regarded Scotch whiskies, has forged a multi-award winning sponsorship partnership with National Museums Scotland. The partnership is based on supporting research into the museum's world class collections from early medieval Scotland (AD 300–900, the period after the Romans and before the Vikings). These have special resonance for Glenmorangie and its brand heritage – its distillery is based in what was a heartland of the ancient and mysterious Pictish people of Scotland.

The six-year bespoke partnership was formed in 2007; Glenmorangie wanted to promote its redesigned brand via a cultural sponsorship which enriched both the brand story and the cultural life of the nation. Brand values were key in the selection process – both organisations share brand values of 'telling stories' and 'making revelations'. The partnership had to have media 'campaignability' and this sponsorship vehicle had huge potential for 'revealing' new discoveries, showing how these mysterious early people reflected their society and beliefs in the sophisticated objects they created.

Glenmorangie adopted a spiral design from a sculptured stone, an eighth-century Pictish masterpiece, as its new brand emblem for a major product re-launch. The stone originally stood near their distillery and is now displayed in the National Museum of Scotland. This inspired the new packaging and design that has successfully transformed Glenmorangie into a luxury brand that has strong resonance with premium spirits drinkers in its global markets.

Key objectives of the sponsorship are:

- enriching the Glenmorangie brand identity and generating stories for release to the media;
- generating Scottish media coverage;

- raising awareness of Glenmorangie's Scottish roots, despite foreign owner-ship (it is part of the Louis Vuitton Moet Hennessy Group);
- generating interest and 'talkability' among Scottish opinion formers;
- providing independent third party endorsement for Glenmorangie;
- enhancing Glenmorangie's status as an active corporate citizen.

Glenmorangie funded a re-evaluation of this key period of the nation's history. Central to this was the creation of a named archaeology post, Glenmorangie Research Officer (the only known sponsored position of its kind).

National Museums Scotland also commissioned Scottish craftspeople to recreate contemporary versions of world renowned treasures from early medi-eval Scotland, resonating with Glenmorangie's values of great craftsmanship rooted in history. Bringing the past alive in this way created stories to tell, enriching Glenmorangie's brand identity and delivering sustained media coverage.

Commissions included the first Pictish throne to be built in over 1,000 years, which captured media attention. Appropriately, it was displayed in the seat of Scottish power – the Scottish Parliament, highlighting Glenmorangie's invest-ment in the nation's cultural life to key influencers. One Member of the Scottish Parliament tabled a motion praising the success of the partnership in shedding light on the little understood but formative period of the Scottish nation, and creating new works of art.

Regular partnership events reached opinion formers, offering a winning combination of inspirational 'intellectual hospitality' and enlightening tutored whisky tastings.

Solutions

The partnership gave the Glenmorangie brand:

- a prolific, sustained profile in the media through regular revelations about new findings;
- a strong sense of identity – the new logo reflecting the partnership appears on all packaging, promoting Glenmorangie's Scottish identity in a way that links it to the nation's intriguing cultural past and is not stereotypical;
- a powerful 'sense of place' and heritage – this was key to the successful brand re-launch;
- stature – early medieval Scotland was a sophisticated society of European significance, chiming with Glenmorangie's luxury brand values;
- an enhanced reputation among opinion formers as an active corporate citizen, investing in the cultural wellbeing of the nation.

The partnership gave National Museums Scotland:

- funding for a full-time dedicated archaeological research post;
- the opportunity to significantly enhance understanding of this important period of Scotland's past and National Museums Scotland's collections which relate to it;

- the opportunity to enhance public understanding of the period through the production of a major book on the subject and an extensive series of lectures and public programmes;
- the opportunity to undertake and publish innovative academic research;
- a range of highly visual opportunities for media coverage concerning National Museums Scotland's activities.

A campaign of regular 'exclusive revelations' about the Pictish craft commissions and research outputs was scheduled. The sponsorship aligned the brand with a project making important discoveries about iconic national treasures, investing in the cultural life of the nation and underlining Glenmorangie's Scottish credentials. The media campaign promoted the brand identity in an authentic and powerful manner.

The scheduled media campaign of two to three key research findings per year, supported by additional ad hoc PR opportunities, delivered a significant profile. Media coverage was quantified as over 60 million opportunities to see, and the advertising and editorial value equivalent was in excess of the sponsorship fee.

The sponsorship has been most successful in: enriching the Glenmorangie brand story; creating engaging stories to deliver significant media exposure; and in its emotional impact on target audiences. Its success is reflected in major sponsorship award wins, acknowledging the innovative nature of the partnership and its delivery of significant benefits for both organisations.

Summary

While this textbook focuses on event sponsorship, it is important to consider other revenue raising opportunities that may provide the necessary support. Some of these may be beneficial to sponsorship partners, such as catering opportunities, and therefore can add value to a sponsor but they can be a revenue stream in themselves.

In many cases these revenue making opportunities would be undertaken by specialist providers who may pay for the rights and based on sales so the funds may be without risk, just a management role.

Discussion questions

1 This chapter aimed to reinforce the idea that traditional sponsorship is only one source of income to realise a project. Do you think it is the easiest way after considering these alternatives?
2 Do you think government funding is only relevant for major events? Outline the rational for government funding.
3 What are the potential problems with merchandise as a revenue source?

Bibliography

(n.d.) Retrieved 25 May 2012, from Artist Share: www.artistshare.net/v4/

Bennett, R. (2003) 'Corporate hospitality: Executive indulgence or vital corporate communications weapon?' *Corporate Communications: An International Journal*, vol. 8, issue 4, pp. 229–240.

Blackshaw, I. (2012) *Sports Marketing Agreements*, Springer, Secaucus, NJ.

Cadbury Australia (n.d.) www.fundraising.com.au/ (retrieved 29 April 2012).

Carne, L. (2012, 13 July) 'McDonalds loses London Olympics chip monopoly'. Retrieved 30 July 2012 from www.news.com.au: www.news.com.au/business/companies/mcdonalds-loses-london-olympics-chip-monopoly

Dove, K. E. (2002) *Conducting a Succesful Major Gift and Planned Giving Program: A Comprehensive Guide and Resource*, Jossey-Bass, San Francisco, CA.

Johnson, G. (2012) 'Outraged supporters turn to online donating', *Fundraising and Philanthropy*, 7 February from http//www.fpmagazine.com.au/outraged-supporters-turn-to-online-donating-298564.

news.com.au. (2012, 12 July) 'Games ban on chips, unless it is with fish'. Retrieved 30 July 2012, from www.news.com.au/business/companies/games-ban-on-chips-unless-its-with-fish

Pegg, C. (2012, 24 April) 'How to stand out with the crowd'. Retrieved 28 May 2012, from *The Australian*: www.theaustralian.com.au/arts/how-to-stand-out-with-the-crowd/story-e6frg8n6-1226336495964

Chapter 10

Trends in sponsorship

Learning outcomes

After reading and discussing the contents of this chapter, students will be able to:

- outline three trends in the future development of sponsorship;
- describe the difference between sponsorship, a corporate social responsibility action and corporate philanthropy;
- describe how ethics impact on sponsorship.

Introduction

For many years organisations have placed increasing pressure on all expenditure lines, constantly tightening budgets, minimising risk and waste, and seeking increased productivity and efficiency. In relation to many sponsorships, the expectations from sponsors and the need to justify costs and level of reporting required have escalated. The amount of resourcing in selling, managing and reporting on sponsorships has increased.

Event marketing has been shown to be an effective form or marketing, and there are examples which demonstrate brands bypassing sponsorship and becoming event producers themselves. This, together with pressure on businesses to consider corporate social philanthropy and ethical practices, are all trends in sponsorship which will develop over time.

Accountability

In many cases it seems budget lines exclusively for brand building have contracted or been deleted and those funds transferred to the product managers to build resources to sell product rather than promote brand. Product managers are far more accountable for their expenditure and on a short time frame evaluation cycle.

For many years sponsorship was treated like traditional advertising in that it was a one-way relationship – logos on display, products in the audience, promotions and sampling for sponsorship and product to consumer for traditional advertising.

In today's world, the online world, marketing and advertising costs in the digital area are far less significant and far more targeted. This is a more effective method of communicating for some organisations. Similarly sustainability, environmental and ethical issues have risen in the public and corporate conscience. Additionally as traditional borders are weakened by digital communication and expenditure is more heavily scrutinised, more programmes are being rolled out globally.

Since the 1970s corporations have faced pressure from a broad range of stakeholders to become more socially responsible. These pressures come from a range of sources but the most significant is consumer activism. These include:

- public scepticism concerning corporate motives, as evidenced by reports of corporate scandal and unethical behaviour (e.g. Enron, Anderson and WorldCom);
- alleged abuse of human rights and exploitative labour policies (e.g. Nike and Levi's);
- economic impact of CSR lapses linked to reputational risk and damage (e.g. Union Carbide, BP);
- potential of consumer boycotts (e.g. Shell) have forced corporations to monitor their social performance closely (Tracey *et al.* 2005).

Sponsorship and corporate social responsibility and corporate philanthropy all share some common principals. These are:

- A business is connected to the society it operates in, or engages with.
- A business needs to connect with its market and create a relationship with it.
- A business faces costs in terms of cash or other resources.

There are other trends appearing, for example:

Blurring of lines

Throughout the world the fast food chain McDonald's supports respite facilities for the parents of children being cared for in hospital. The facility, 'Ronald McDonald House', is a wonderful and needed facility.

It is not regarded as sponsorship but as a part of McDonald's commitment to society and is an example of corporate social responsibility; however, the line is fairly grey in that the naming rights of the facility no doubt provide brand reinforcement about McDonald's, resulting in the commitment as having a positive brand or marketing outcome.

Corporate television programming

McDonald's has taken the next step in advertising – they are now producing television programmes. This bypasses other regulatory or content controls. Broadcasters, be they pay or free to air, are looking for ways to access content that is cost effective – how better than to have someone make it for you so all you have to do is screen it!

McDonald's Gets Grilled airs on Channel Seven in Australia. The film is the boldest example yet of a growing genre: programs funded by advertisers that help content-hungry TV stations fill their schedules. McDonald's and the production company insist the show is not an ad, a view challenged by some producers.

They say it is an 'access all areas investigation' that puts the McDonald's business under the 'microscope'. It follows six volunteers as they visit suppliers nominated by the company, including small vegetable farmers in Australia, as well as chicken giant Ingham and frozen food company McCain.

McDonald's insists it did not impose any editorial control and the people recruited by the production company were unaware of the program's nature until shooting began. The only payment they received was a daily allowance.

The McDonald's chief executive in Australia, Catriona Noble, said the show was an exercise in citizen journalism and a chance for people 'to ask the tough questions and get honest answers, independently of McDonald's'.

She said it did not consider allowing a current affairs filmmaker access: because the public was more likely to relate to people like themselves than journalists.

But it is the disclosure of the relationship that is likely to be the most contentious issue. In the film's opening minute, the host says that 'McDonald's commissioned an independent production company' and Channel Seven is planning its own disclosure.

But because Channel Seven did not pay for the program, nor was it paid [for] by McDonald's, the program is not covered by the Australian TV industry's code of practice and the media regulator, the Australian Communications and Media Authority, would not comment until it had seen the show.

The body representing production companies was in no doubt: 'From our point of view, it's an advertorial and not a documentary', Geoff Brown, the executive director of the Screen Producers Association of Australia, said.

Advertiser-funded TV is set to take off here after successes in the US where shows such as Earth 2050, funded by Shell and run on the Discovery Channel and Joga Bonito, a film about football and funded by Nike, achieved respectable ratings.

(Lee 2012)

Brands that invent their own events

The traditional model for sponsorship is also challenged when would-be sponsors decide to produce the event themselves. Traditionally event producers would approach prospective sponsors to align themselves to the event and in return for the benefits (outlined in earlier chapters of this book) they pay the event producer.

Projects such as The Creators Project and the Red Bull Air Race are two examples where the prospective sponsor has moved to the role of producer.

The Creators Project

The Creators Project was born from a global partnership between Intel, the computer component manufacturer and Vice, a youth media company that includes publishing, events, music, digital television, marketing and feature film divisions.

Launched in 2010, The Creators Project is an ongoing multi-year programme that is dedicated to identifying leading artists and enabling them to showcase their works and artistic visions through technology and interactive media. The programme includes 'The Studio', an international event series, a documentary TV series, multi-disciplinary collaborative projects and the video web site, TheCreatorsProject.com.

In just one year, The Creators Project has become a cultural phenomenon. Tens of thousands of guests have attended the events, and the content was viewed over 55 million times online.

The project unites a vast collection of artists, designers, musicians and filmmakers who are using technology to push the bounds of creative expression. To date, there are more than 100 Creators involved, hailing mostly from seven countries (United States, United Kingdom, Germany, France, Brazil, South Korea and China) along with other artists from around the world.

Together the two companies met over a shared passion for art and creativity and a common belief that there was a better way of elevating artists and supporting new work with them.

The founders of *Vice* magazine did not feel there were the appropriate platforms of outlets for creativity and set out to create a voice and a venue they could call their own. It was digital technology that turned the ambition into a reality. For example, things like the innovations in desktop publishing which were instrumental in allowing the birth of *Vice* magazine in the early 1990s. Today, low cost digital filmmaking, post production and high speed online distribution have democratised the worlds of film and television. Without these innovations VBS.TV would not have been possible and *Vice* would not have made the shift from print to video.

> At the heart of this ongoing revolution is Intel. No matter what field of human endeavour you look at – science, sport, commerce, communications and media, the arts – it would be hard to imagine the last several decades of global human striving without the advent of digital computing technologies. By the same token it would be virtually impossible to imagine modern computing without Intel. Intel chips, housed deep inside the computers and devices that we touch every day, have been the secret hearts bringing our new world to life. Intel processor

technology and their steadfast belief in a better future has supported creators of all kinds, in all fields, from day one.

(The Creators Project)

How is this an emerging trend?

In recent years an event producer might look to Intel for sponsorship of events that showcase or create brand marketing opportunities; although much of Intel's budget is directed to The Creators Project. The Creators Project enhances other events with its amazing work but it comes fully programmed rather than providing direct investment to the event; for example, The Creators Project was part of Coachella Festival in USA and Vivid Festival in Australia.

Deborah Conrad, Intel vice president and chief marketing officer, said:

> We knew we had a great idea last year when we worked with *Vice* to kick off The Creators Project, but we didn't really quite wrap our heads around the magnitude of the global appetite for innovation. This comes from the collision of art and technology. Last year, we celebrated a new generation of creative and artistic geniuses. And in our second year, we'll continue the celebration, but evolve the program to become a patron for the creative process, such as adding The Studio and a partnership with Coachella. We're going bigger, better, richer and deeper in 2011 to empower even more creators in unimaginable ways. Prepare to be wowed.

(The Creators Project)

Red Bull Air Race

The Red Bull Air Race was conceived in 2001 in the Red Bull sports think-tank which has been responsible for creating a range of new sports events across the world. Red Bull is an energy drink made in Austria but with its origins in Thailand. It is the biggest selling energy drink in the world.

The aim of the event was to develop a new aviation race that would challenge the ability of the world's best pilots, creating a race in the sky that was not simply about speed, but also precision and skill. The answer was to build a specially designed obstacle course which the pilots would navigate at high speeds. It was also aimed at building or reinforcing Red Bull as an energy drink and aligning itself to the company tag line 'Red Bull gives you wings'.

Development of the prototypes of what are now known as the 'Air Gates' (20-metre-high inflatable markers) began in 2002 and renowned Hungarian pilot Péter Besenyei successfully completed the first test flight through them. The first official Red Bull Air Race was held in Austria in 2003 and the second was staged later the same year in Hungary.

The event grew from strength to strength, leading to being staged as the Red Bull Air Race World Series. Ten pilots competed in seven races around the world.

Eight races took place in 2006 with 11 pilots competing; in 2007 the calendar was extended to include ten races with the first race on South American soil taking place in

Rio de Janeiro. Twelve pilots took part in 2008 in eight races around the globe. The largest number of pilots so far took part in six races in 2009, and 15 pilots from 12 different countries competed for the world championship title.

During training runs prior to the race in the 2010 series a Brazilian pilot crashed his plane into the Swan River in Perth. Rescuers were on site within seconds and the pilot was rushed to Royal Perth Hospital where it was determined that he had suffered no serious injury. As of 2013, it is the only crash in the history of the Red Bull Air Race.

This event is owned, run and managed by Red Bull similarly to The Creators Project, the Red Bull Air Race being an event owned by the company, rather than sponsored by Red Bull. This trend, where sponsors or potential sponsors undertake their own event marketing activities, seems to be increasing.

Cause-related marketing

Depending on your event or project, cause-related marketing might also be worth considering as a revenue source. As the name implies, it tends to be applied to a 'cause' and some form of social outcome; nevertheless, if the project is right the model might be applied more broadly.

Cause-related marketing is the name given to marketing which involves a collaborative relationship between a 'for profit' business and a 'non-profit' business. The term is sometimes used more broadly and generally to refer to any type of marketing effort for social and other charitable causes, including in-house marketing efforts by non-profit organisations. Some of the best case studies involve medical research, environmental and educational causes.

Case study 10.1

Mount Franklin Spring Water and breast cancer (McGrath Foundation)

One of the leading brands of bottled spring water in Australia is Mount Franklin. One the most high profile public health issues is breast cancer.

Mount Franklin's cause-related marketing campaign involves two major elements, first in donating $250,000 to the McGrath Foundation (McGrath Foundation 2012) in 2010 to help fund McGrath breast care nurses in communities right across Australia; and second to help educate young women to be breast aware. The education is in part through Mount Franklin changing its packaging for Breast Cancer Awareness Month by turning the lids of the bottles from their usual blue to pink: 'Pink will be on everyone's lips this October, with Mount Franklin turning its lids pink once again to celebrate Breast Cancer Awareness Month in support of the McGrath Foundation.'

The McGrath Foundation was established in 2003 following the cancer diagnosis of Jane McGrath, wife of leading Australian cricketer Glenn McGrath, who has used his profile and networks to build the Foundation profile. For some time pink has been adopted by breast cancer campaigners as being their signature colour and over time this has been embraced by the general community.

To consumers facing refrigerators full of different branded bottled spring waters the point of difference is an important driver, as many people are directly or indirectly aware of breast cancer. Knowing that the purchase of Mount Franklin over the competitors' products will assist in the care of breast cancer sufferers and in research into the disease gives the consumer the incentive that makes the difference – aside from taste differences which most would agree are minimal.

Mount Franklin has demonstrated that its commitment to the issue is genuine and not exclusively commercial as the brand has been associated with the support of breast cancer charities since 2006, when it first turned its bottles pink for the National Breast Cancer Foundation. In 2010 Mount Franklin formed a new partnership with the McGrath Foundation and since 2006 the brand has contributed more than $1.5 million to the cause.

Tracy Bevan, executive director of the McGrath Foundation, said that the Mount Franklin pink lids on the market in October 2012 was another sign of the growing breadth of McGrath Foundation support and another example of a McGrath Foundation 'Corporate Friend' using their marketing clout to help spread the Foundation's message of breast awareness and support.

Mount Franklin undertook a major marketing launch to help promote its new partnership with the McGrath Foundation. Mount Franklin products will be provided to various McGrath Foundation community events, further supporting the Foundation's strong ties to community-driven initiatives (Release n.d.).

Ethical issues

Ethical issues are going to continually challenge event producers or sponsorship seekers. These are situations where a prospective sponsor is using the sponsorship to minimise other public or government interference (regulatory issues). In the last 30 years in some countries probably the best example was tobacco sponsorship. While tobacco sponsorship or advertising is not banned globally, it is banned from many countries. Tobacco sponsorship was largely directed at sports, fashion and the arts. The alignment of sporting fitness with tobacco, of singing virtuosity with tobacco, and glamour and beauty with tobacco was a useful foil by the tobacco industry until the government (regulators) made such sponsorship illegal.

Other industries are also under fire for testing ethical issues with alignments such as fast foods with children, or alcohol with music and sport.

Recently the International Olympic Committee welcomed the entry of Dow Chemical as a TOP level sponsor. There was significant negative media coverage of Dow's sponsorship due to its association with the industrial disaster in Bhopal 1984 where a poisonous gas leaked from the tanks of the Union Carbide pesticide plant located in the Cholla area of Bhopal on the night of 2–3 December 1984, killing more than 20,000 people and maiming thousands more for life. Dow, which acquired Union Carbide, has refused to increase a $470 million compensation package that it agreed to in 1989.

So incensed were the community that a 'Special' Olympics was held for the affected children. Children aged 5–16, cheered by their friends and families, participated in ten sports in Bhopal during the 'Special' Olympics. The move was aimed to attract attention to the responsibilities of the company, which has a contract with the IOC until 2020 and, in particular, was a sponsor of the London Olympics (Dutta 2012). It seems that the London Organising Committee were conscious that the sponsorship might cause negative publicity, as a motion to terminate the sponsorship was narrowly rejected by 11 votes to 10 by the committee (Pino and Kannel 2012).

Event organisations will come under more scrutiny from the perspective of environmental sustainability in years to come.

The following is a vignette illustrating another ethical issue.

Vignette: Dungog Film Festival

In a rural town in Australia called Dungog, a regional film festival was struggling to secure an income stream from a private donor or corporate sponsor which together with box office income and limited government support would fund the project. The film festival programme focused on Australian films, which made it different from other film festivals.

The surrounding areas around Dungog were farming lands but were being looked at with increasing interest by various mining interests which could see value in the mineral resources that could potentially be mined.

The New South Wales Mineral Council, the peak body in New South Wales representing the mining industry, came forward as the major sponsor – confirming their commitment to the cultural wellbeing of the area. There was an outcry from the community because many people saw the partnership as 'selling out' to the mining industry and suggested that the sponsorship was intended to merely buy goodwill from the community.

'Festival or mineral: sponsorship tension'

Miners and filmmakers have far more in common than most people suppose, according to the Minerals Council of NSW.

They are 'innovative, sensible, ingenious, and unconventional, using metaphorical blood and tears to enrich our lives with what I would call "mineral magic",' said the chief executive of the Minerals Council, Nikki Williams, at the launch of the Dungog Film Festival.

The festival, which opened last night in the Hunter Valley town, has the state's peak mining body as its major sponsor, but some in the community feel the event is being dominated by coal interests.

The *Sydney Morning Herald* spoke to Dungog residents, including some volunteering with the festival, who are disturbed by what they see as the intrusion. Disgruntled filmmakers are also staging a fringe festival, screening environmental documentaries, to highlight some of the effects of long wall coal mining.

The Minerals Council sponsorship of the event is part of a wider public relations push by the mining industry to counter perceptions about the industry's role in climate change and environmental damage.

Guests at the Sydney launch of the Dungog Festival last month were handed booklets urging people to 'forget the hype' around mining.

The Dungog festival's director, Allannah Zitserman, said she was willing to discuss the Mineral Council's role in the event but later could not be reached for comment.

One filmmaker the *Herald* spoke to believed that talking about mining might compromise the festival's funding.

'It would be nice if they could just sponsor us instead of trying to brainwash us as well,' the filmmaker said.

A Dungog resident, Helen Graham, said she attended the opening of the festival last year to watch films and rapidly became uncomfortable with the number of mining references.

'Then they had the hide to have a couple of younger people stand up and talk about being a mine employee as though it was the greatest job in the world. I just felt really sick . . . They were just using the festival for a lot of PR.'

People from the council are also staffing the box office, answering phones and helping out with publicity, Dr Williams said. 'Without the amount of volunteers we have provided, it's hard to see the event getting off the ground,' she said.

'There really is nothing suspicious about it, we want to support this community in every way and help out.'

(Cubby 2009)

As an event producer, how would you deal with this issue?

Crowd source funding

Crowd source funding is a direct approach to individuals though online appeals. Of all the alternatives to sponsorship, crowd source funding is the most significant new funding method. It has come about as our lives have become increasingly influenced by the online world.

'Crowd source' funding or 'crowdfunding' denotes the collective co-operation, attention and trust by people who network and pool their money and other resources together, to support efforts initiated by other people or organisations.

The event, product or cause that the funds are being attracted to support may be commercial or community driven activities and there are great examples of each. Web sites such as Kickstarter, Pozible, ArtistShare and Sponsume all offer the platform to seek financial support/investment/donations to allow projects to be realised.

In 1997, fans underwrote an entire US tour for the British rock group Marillion (http://ipledg.com/help/school/what-is-crowd-funding) and managed to raise $60,000 with donations following a fan-based Internet campaign. The idea was conceived and managed by the fans before any involvement by the band.

The United States-based company ArtistShare (Artist Share) (2000/2001) is documented as being the first crowdfunding web site for music, followed later by sites such as Sellaband (2006), IndieGoGo (2008), Pledge Music (2009), Kickstarter (2009), RocketHub (2009), and in the UK Sponsume (2010).

There is a significant difference in the motivations and expectations of a crowd source funding campaign driven towards a commercial outcome as outlined above compared to those driven towards a community or philanthropic outcome as discussed below. Nevertheless the model is not significantly different and there are great examples of both.

As the use of online platforms grows so do the terms used to describe them; for example micro patronage. This is a system in which the public directly supports the work of others by making donations through the Internet. To take an everyday example, an email request to sponsor a friend in a fun run or other endeavour might be seen as micro patronage. Micro patronage differs from traditional patronage systems by allowing many 'patrons' to donate small amounts, rather than a small number of patrons making larger contributions.

Crowdfunding philanthropy has emerged to allow ordinary web users to support specific philanthropic projects without the need for large amounts of money. Global Giving allows individuals to browse through a selection of small projects proposed by non-profit organisations worldwide, and donate funds to projects of their choice. Microcredit crowdfunding platforms such as Kiva (organisation) and Wokai facilitate crowdfunding of loans managed by microcredit organisations in developing countries. The US-based non-profit Zidisha offers a new twist on these themes, applying a direct person-to-person lending model to microcredit lending for low-income small business owners in developing countries. Zidisha borrowers who pass a background check may post microloan applications directly on the Zidisha web site, specifying proposed credit terms and interest rates.

> Brisbane artist Jason Bray is happy to report he may never have to apply for a government arts grant again.
>
> The filmmaker was one of several people sharing their experiences in Brisbane at a public forum last week on crowdfunding – the increasingly popular practice of securing pooled donations online. Organised by Australian creative crowdfunding website Pozible, the event forms part of the platform's push to redefine how Australians think about and fund the arts.
>
> Pozible co-founder Alan Crabbe says crowdfunding has turned the tables on the passive exercise of waiting for grants as almost half of the website's traffic is generated by social media use. Bray's documentary Street Dreams, about Southeast Asia's prostitution trade, is one of about 500 Australian projects that have secured $2 million collectively since Pozible's launch in May 2010.
>
> 'It's empowering creatives to do their own work and not be limited by governments to provide the grants or facilities or resources to do it,' Crabbe says.
>
> 'A lot of artists would say they have to wait around, and there's a lot of unknowns, but being able to get out there and do your own projects without having to shape the project to suit other people or organisations is probably the most valuable asset of running your own campaign.'
>
> Crowd source funding allows artists to bypass the usual funding models and appeal directly to the consumer for support. Elliott Bledsoe, digital content officer at the Australia Council, says the audience-focused nature of the platform is appealing for many artists.

'Rather than trying to convince an arm's length peer assessment board about the merit of a project, you're trying to convince the people who will ultimately press play, or sit in a seat and watch it on stage or whatever. I think it presents a very different way of thinking about how you plan a project that you're hoping to deliver,' Bledsoe says.

[. . .]

Pozible's early successes were modest, but within a few months the struggling website New Matilda secured $175,000 in just 50 days, which remains the platform's biggest project to date.

[. . .]

'The biggest way it differs to a government agency or an NGO funding you is that you really feel the support of the people,' he (Bledsoe) says. 'You don't write an amazingly good grant application and then one person decides "yes, that is worth it, we're going to acknowledge that and support that". It's a collective, unanimous voice.'

(Pegg 2012)

The online world operates very quickly, as the following case outlines, and not always favourably!

Outraged supporters turn to online donating

A controversy over funding between two non-profit organisations in the United States of America has demonstrated how social media and on-line giving can mobilise an army of unhappy supporters to donate. Planned Parenthood launched an immediate social media and email marketing campaign to its supporters when the Susan G. Komen Foundation announced it would stop its grants that enabled breast cancer examinations and information.

Supporters were angered by the news, which it was speculated – though vigorously denied – resulted from pressure by pro-life organisations (Planned Parenthood also provides abortion advice and services). A flurry of donations ensued from irate supporters.

Just 24 hours after the story broke, the *Washington Post* reported that Planned Parenthood had received over US$400,000 from 6,000 donors – well on the way to replacing funding that had totalled $580,000 from the Susan G. Komen Foundation in the previous year.

(Johnson 2012)

Marketing engine drives backlash

While the Susan G. Komen Foundation remained silent as it scrambled to come up with a response to the PR disaster, Planned Parenthood was busy driving home the consequences of the funding withdrawal through social media and traditional press. Its well-oiled advocacy machine made the most of the radio silence, driving home what the funding withdrawal would mean for the provision of a vital women's health service.

Amongst the donors to get on board was New York mayor Michael Bloomberg, who pledged to match gifts dollar for dollar up to US$250,000. By the time Susan G. Komen Foundation succumbed to the public pressure and reversed its funding decision three days later, Planned Parenthood had reported over US$3 million in donations from across the country.

When it issued a press release regarding the funding reversal, Planned Parenthood was brilliant in reporting back to and thanking its supporters for their efforts:

> Every dollar we received for this fund will go directly for breast exams and diagnostic services, as well as breast health outreach and education. And now that the Komen Foundation plans to continue their support, even more women will receive lifesaving breast cancer care.
>
> We look forward to continuing our partnership with Komen partners, leaders, and volunteers, and supporters like you. Thank you so much for your voice and for standing with us.
>
> (Johnson 2012)

Bizzare sponsorship

Standing out from the crowd will always be a quality sponsors are looking for – similarly corporate hospitality companies are looking at being the first and standing out from the crowd. Sometimes this has a great outcome, while at others it backfires. It was reported in trade magazine *B&T* (Sandev 2012) that Mini Cooper, the car brand, paid US$370 to sponsor a storm in Europe – namely rainy weather with thunder and lightning. The storm was known as Cooper and it led to 70 deaths and 500 people being hospitalised. The sponsorship was developed by a Munich-based advertising agency, Sassenbach – Germany and the United States of America are the only countries that condone the practice of selling the naming rights to high- and low-pressure weather systems.

Summary

This chapter has looked at a few trends but there are many others that could have been explored. Sponsorship as an industry is constantly evolving and as an applied study it is influenced by many external elements such as general economic climate, cyclical approaches to global or local marketing campaigns and issues such as ethics and corporate social responsibility. These can vary from territory to territory and with corporate and political leaders, and as our media change, so do the tools we have to secure, develop and promote sponsors.

Discussion questions

1 Do you believe more corporates are building their own events?
2 Explain what projects might be *best* supported via crowd source funding.
3 What about the ethics of the Dungog vignette? Would you have accepted the support?

Bibliography

(n.d.) Retrieved 28 May 2012, from I Pledge: http://ipledg.com/help/school/what-is-crowd-funding

(n.d.a) Retrieved 25 May 2012, from Artist Share: www.artistshare.net/v4/

The Creators Project dramatically expands in 2011; launches major studio to produce world's leading artists, from: http://newsroom.intel.com/community/intel/blog/2011/02/23the-creators-project-dramatically-expands-in-2011-launches-major-studio-to-produce-worlds-leading-artists.

Cubby, B. (2009) 'Festival or mineral: Sponsorship tension', *Sydney Morning Herald*, 29 May.

Dutta, A. (2012) 'Bhopal gas tragedy victims fume at Bachchan's Olympics run', 29 July. Retrieved 30 July 2012, from *India Today*: http:indiatoday.intoday.in/story/olympics-amitabh-bachchan-torch-run bhopal-gas-tragedy

Johnson, G. (2012) 'Outraged supporters turn to online donating', *Fundraising and Philanthropy*, 7 February, from: http://www.fpmagazine.com.au/outraged-supporters-turn-to-online-donating-298564/

Lee, J. (2012) 'Mcdonalds finds another channel to take its story to the market', *Sydney Morning Herald*, 31 March, www.smh.com.au/business/media-and-marketing/mcdonalds-finds-another-channel-to-take-its-story-to-the-market-20120330–1w3m9.html#ixzz1vN94QVn9

McGrath Foundation (2012) *Spring forward with Mount Franklin Pink Lids*. Retrieved 30 July 2012, from McGrath Foundation: www.mcgrathfoundation.com.au/

Pegg, C. (2012) 'How to stand out with the crowd', 24 April. Retrieved 28 May 2012, from *The Australian*: www.theaustralian.com.au/arts/how-to-stand-out-with-the-crowd/story-e6frg8n6–1226336495964

Pino, I. and Kannel, C. with Gardner, T. M. (2012) 'How Dow Chemical can end the Bhopal tragedy', 27 July. Retrieved 30 July 2012, from *Daily Finance*: www.dailyfinance.com/2012/07/27/how-dow-chemical-can-end-the-bhopal-tragedy

Release, Coca-Cola Amatil (n.d.) Sydney, NSW, Australia.

Sandev, M. (2012) 'Frosty reception for Mini Cooper promo stunt', 3 February, *B&T*, 2, www.bandt.com.au/. . ./frosty-reception-for-mini-cooper-promo-stunt

The Creators Project (n.d.) *The Creators Project dramatically expands in 2011; launches major studio to produce world's leading artists*, from: http://newsroom.intel.com/community/intel/blog/2011/02/23the-creators-project-dramatically-expands-in-2011-launches-major-studio-to-produce-worlds-leading-artists.

Tracey, P., Phillips, N. and Haugh, H. (2005) 'Beyond philanthropy: Community enterprise as a basis for corporate citizenship', *Journal of Business Ethics*, vol. 58, no. 4, pp. 327–344.

Index

Note: Tables are indicated in bold; figures in italics.